IAN GITTINS

BJÖRK

THERE'S MORE TO LIFE THAN THIS

THE STORIES BEHIND EVERY SONG

BJORK: THERE'S MORE TO LIFE THAN THIS

Text copyright © 2002 Ian Gittins
Design copyright © 2002 Carlton Books Limited

Published by
Thunder's Mouth Press
161 William St., 16th Floor
New York, NY 10038

Published in Great Britain by Carlton Books Limited
20 Mortimer Street
London
W1T 3JW

Library of Congress Cataloging-in-Publication Data

Gittins, Ian
        Björk: there's more to life than this / by Ian Gittins.
            p.cm.
        Includes discography (p.) and index.
        ISBN 1-56025-416-5 (trade paper)
1. Björk. 2. Women rock musicians – Biography.   I. Title

        ML420.B599 G58 2002
        782.42164'092 –dc21
        [B]

            2002072433

ISBN 1-56025-416-5

9 8 7 6 5 4 3 2 1

Executive Editor: Sarah Larter
Senior Art Editor: Diane Spender
Editor: Mike Flynn
Design: Michael Spender
Picture Research: Adrian Bentley,
Stephen O'Kelly
Production: Sarah Corteel
Jacket Design: Alison Tutton

Printed in Dubai
Distributed by Publishers Group West

PICTURE CREDITS

The publishers would like to thank the following sources
for their kind permission to reproduce the pictures in
this book:

All Action/Olly Hewitt 49, J/Thomas 61, 71, 74, 76,
83, 91, 93, 138, John Gladwin 62, 66, 77, Doug Peters
89, Andy Willsher 95, Duncan Raban 139.
**The Kobal Collection/ARTE FRANCE/BLIND
SPOT/DINOVI** 112
London Features International /Anthony Pidgeon 70,
Caroline Torem-Craig 141, Geoff Swaine 132, Gie
Knaeps 97, Gregg De Guire 115, Rick Georgeson 124,
Ron Wolfson 53.
Redferns/David Redfern 90, Fotex/ST.Malzorn 86 ,
Mick Hutson 46, 50, 57, 68/9, Patrick Ford 81 Robin
Little 82
Retna/Chris Talyor 85, Darren Filkins 75, Niels Van
Iperen 41, 44, 129, Wendy Idele 4, 130/1.
Rex 25, 29, 32, 34/5, 42, 94, 99, 100,104, 107,
109, 122, 126, 127, 101, 141, Brain Rasic 59,
Aslan/Niviere 118, Charles Sykes 119, Grunewald
134,Huw Evans 106, M.Le.Pour Trench 33, Meicneux
123, Munawar Hosain 117 Nils Jorgensen 120, Ricardo
Lopez 87, Richard Young 40, 56,135, Stephen Sweet
34, 55, Steward Cook 113, The Sun 9, 10, 11, 12, 14,
15, 17, 19, 140, Tom Stockhill 30, 65, Y.Lenquette 21.
S.I.N/ Anthony Medley 3, Steve Double 80, Eye
Contact 7, 136, Phil Nicholls 37, Stewart Cook 79, Ian
T.Tilton 133, Jan Tilton 39, Oriita Sourander 20, Peter
Anderson 20/1,
121, 140, Tony Mott 27, 47.
Topfoto/UPPA 102, 110/1, 111

Every effort has been made to acknowledge correctly
and contact the source and/or copyright holder of each
picture, and Carlton Books Limited apologises for any
unintentional errors or omissions which will be
corrected in future editions of this book.

IAN GITTINS

BJÖRK

THERE'S MORE TO LIFE THAN THIS

THE STORIES BEHIND EVERY SONG

THUNDER'S
MOUTH
PRESS

CONTENTS

INTRODUCTION

"I'VE ALWAYS SUNG EVER SINCE I WAS A LITTLE KID," BJÖRK REFLECTED ONCE, ASKED TO EXPLAIN THE APPEAL THAT MUSIC HOLDS FOR HER. "IT'S JUST ALWAYS BEEN MY NATURAL REACTION TO THINGS." THERE IS NO BETTER STARTING-PLACE FOR ANYBODY ATTEMPTING TO DEFINE THE SINGULAR AND MAVERICK MUSE OF BJÖRK GUDMUNDSDÓTTIR.

Björk's sheer, visceral love of music and her delight in experimentation have always marked Iceland's prime cultural export down as a unique talent. From the moment that her first solo album *Debut* launched her to world fame in 1993, she's been correctly regarded as a groundbreaking artist who is manifestly determined to succeed on her own terms only.

Even before *Debut*, though, Björk had demonstrated her singular musical vision, via an album made at a precocious 11 years of age and, of course, contrary art-punks The Sugarcubes. Over the last decade, she's simply established a reputation as arguably the most contrary and compelling pop mega-star on the planet.

Björk, then, is truly a star like no other, with a fascinating and idiosyncratic oeuvre of work that any artist would be proud to own but few would have the wit or originality to create, and from pre-teen folk songs to the colossal *Vespertine*, this is her musical journey to date.

1977

BJÖRK

01 *Björk – The Album*
02 Arabadrengurinn
03 Búkolla
04 Alta Mira
05 Jóhannes Kjarvalv
06 Fúsi Hreindyr
07 Himnaför
08 Óliver
09 Álfur Út Úr Hól
10 Músastiginn
11 Bænin

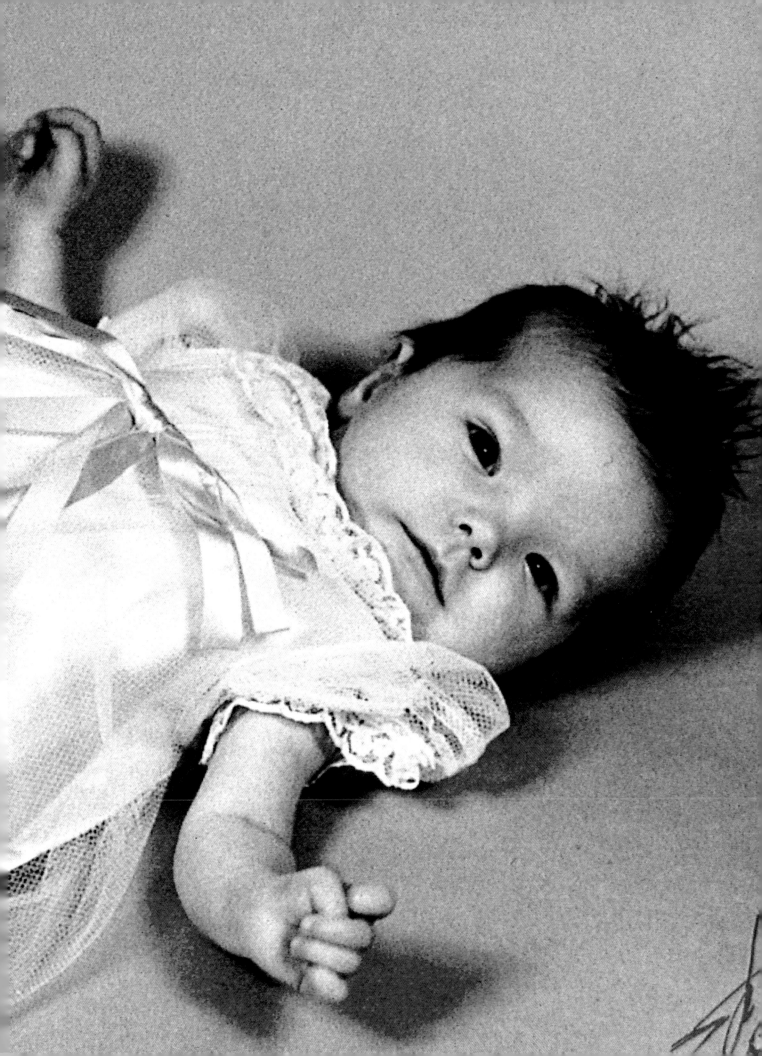

BJÖRK GUDMUNDSDÓTTIR WAS BORN IN REYKJAVIK, THE ICELANDIC CAPITAL, ON NOVEMBER 21, 1965. HER FATHER, ELECTRICAL ENGINEER AND UNION LEADER GUDMUNDUR GUNNARSSON, AND HIS OFFICE WORKER WIFE HILDUR HAUKSDÓTTIR, HAD BEEN MARRIED FOR ONLY A FEW MONTHS. WITH BIZARRELY SCANT REGARD FOR WINDSWEPT ICELAND'S ALMOST TOTAL LACK OF ARBOREAL LIFE, THE COUPLE NAMED THEIR DAUGHTER BJÖRK — "BIRCH TREE".

a headstrong dreamer who, even at this early stage, was showing marked signs of precocity.

"One day I decided I couldn't be bothered to get up and get dressed to go to school," Björk has recollected to numerous interviewers over the years. "So I just cut a hole in my bed sheet for my head and wore it to my lessons. That was normal for me."

Now, it's frequently necessary to ready a largish pinch of salt before accepting all of Björk's outlandish anecdotes at face value. In Martin Aston's engaging *Björkgraphy* (Simon & Schuster, 1996), Hildur rubbished many of her daughter's claims about her enlightened early years. "There were few hippies in Iceland," she laughed, "and I certainly wasn't one of them!"

It can safely be established, however, that by the time Björk was four, Hildur had re-married. Björk's stepfather was to be Sævar Árnason, the guitarist in a local band named Pops. The family home would often host late-night jamming sessions as Reykjavik's rock community congregated at Sævar's, with Björk a willing and intrigued attendee.

Gudmundur and Hildur were scarcely out of their teens when they wed, and within three years of Björk's birth they had divorced. Björk, however, was anything but the textbook damaged, angst-ridden product of a broken home. The parting was entirely amicable, and Björk spent her childhood years contentedly alternating between her mother's and father's households.

"They were really blissful times," she has recalled, evaluating her formative years. "But then, I've always been a happy little idiot."

Björk has routinely described her mother, in interviews, as a "feminist, a rebel and a hippy", and the fledgling star grew up in a shared apartment, which Hildur rented along with various musicians, poets and assorted local bohemians. This liberal environment proved an ideal nurturing ground for

There were already signs that music exerted an unusual fascination over school age Björk. Able to sing the whole of *The Sound Of Music* from the age of three, she attended music college at five. Lessons on the recorder, oboe and piano followed, although young Ms Gudmundsdóttir reserved her greatest enthusiasm for singing. "She started to sing very early," Hildur recalled to Martin Aston.

She may have had no choice. In the early 1970s Iceland offered little to the eager-minded youngster seeking external stimulation and entertainment. "The television only broadcast six days per week, for three hours per day," Björk has recalled. "There was no TV at all on Thursdays, so we'd listen to stories on the radio or read stories to each other. That was our version of computer games!"

However, in 1976 Björk enjoyed the nearest thing that Reykjavik could muster to a big break. An Icelandic radio station commissioned a documentary on her music school. Björk starred as the college's most talented vocal pupil, singing a version of a corny disco tune named 'I Love To Love' that had been a UK hit for Tina Charles. As a result of the broadcast, Björk Gudmundsdóttir got the chance to record an album for a local label, Fálkinn. She was just eleven years old.

01
Björk – The Album

Recorded in a mere fortnight in late 1977, *Björk* is a surprisingly eclectic and accomplished album for one so young. It may be stretching things to claim that Björk's later genius is already evident in these sketchy, precocious tunes, but the record is certainly no disgrace and remains worthy of respectful attention.

Taking two weeks off school, Björk went into Hlidrijinn Studios in Reykjavik to record her Fálkinn-financed album in determined mood. Having been exposed from an early age to creative musical jamming sessions in her family home, the pre-teen fledgling star was to prove no malleable pop puppet.

"The record label offered me all these songs and I turned them down because they were shit," Björk recalled years later to UK monthly music magazine *Q*. "I got upset in the end so my mom got her hippie musician mates to come up with songs for me."

These "hippie musician mates" provided Björk's musical support and bedrock. Sævar, her stepfather, played guitar while local musicians Pálmi Gunnarsson and Sigurdur Karlsson handled production duties. This extended musical family also provided some original material alongside a few corny cover versions, Icelandic folk songs set to pop rhythms and, tellingly, an instrumental written by Björk herself.

Released in time for Iceland's 1977 Christmas market, in a cover which showed Björk sitting cross-legged surrounded by Middle Eastern artefacts and paraphernalia, *Björk* remains a fascinating document and an insight into a highly precocious talent, from the first track onward.

02
Arabadrengurinn

Björk's first-ever recorded song is a jaunty, quasi-Europop tune written by her stepfather, Sævar, and sung, as is the rest of the album, in Icelandic.

Translated as 'Arab Boy', 'Arabadrengurinn' opens with a burst of birdsong and some diligently exotic Eastern strings before quickly transmuting into a bouncy, chirpy electro-ditty. Lyrically, it's a fairytale account of a young girl from Iceland who holidays in Egypt and meets a young Arabian boy on a Cairo night train. He "sings of the water in the oasis and rivers" and "draws pictures with magic lines."

Unsurprisingly, the young girl falls in love with her romantic suitor but they part tearfully at a railway station, never to meet again. Nevertheless, the chorus looks back on a blissfully happy day together spent, oddly, atop a camel: "We went down the Nile/We didn't need a car/Just a dromedary."

'Arabadrengurinn' is a piece of enjoyable fluff, but Björk's vocal performance is engaging and instantly recognizable in its idiosyncratic, tilted delivery and she discharges her childish tale with rare authority, even maintaining her precocious panache as an excruciatingly cheesy organ solo brings the song to its conclusion.

03 Búkolla

'Búkolla' is somewhat of a novelty song, being a bastardization of an Icelandic folk story set to the tune of 'Your Kiss Is Sweet', a soul-pop hit co-written by Stevie Wonder at the height of his 1970s creative purple patch.

'Your Kiss Is Sweet' was written by Wonder together with his protégée Syreeta Wright for her 1974 sophomore album *Stevie Wonder Presents Syreeta*. The original was a piece of classy, chart-friendly bubblegum funk that doubtless came to the young Björk's attention when it was a worldwide hit on Tamla Motown in early 1975.

Björk retains the tune from the Syreeta song but entirely rewrites the lyrics. Búkolla is the name of a cow in an old Icelandic saga, and this song finds Björk and the "cowsy-wowsy" running from two pursuing Icelandic ogres, pausing only to see first a fire and then a mountain spring up from a hair from the cow's tail left on the ground.

The lyric could hardly be in starker contrast to Wonder's sentimental, saccharine original, and 'Búkolla' is lent a cartoon-like air by Björk's ingenuous, infant tones and Pálmi Gunnarsson's comedic trampoline-style bass riff. It's a whimsical, surrealist oddity, and ultimately rather sweet.

04 Alta Mira

It's not hard to discern the influence of Björk's blues-loving stepfather Sævar behind her decision to cover 'Alta Mira', an anthem by early 1970s Texas-based roots rockers the Edgar Winter Group.

Edgar Winter was a multi-instrumentalist jazz and rock-loving bluesman who recorded with his brother Johnny before forming his own band in 1972. 'Alta Mira' appeared on his 1973 album *They Only Come Out At Night*, which also spawned his most famous track, the lairy, sprawling May 1973 US number one hit 'Frankenstein'.

By Winters' usual intense standards the singalong 'Alta Mira' was virtually a lounge croon throwaway, and Björk unsurprisingly renders it as even more of a party tune. She sounds like she's having big fun as she repeatedly yodels the tune's chorus and the perky timpani lends the song a distinct Caribbean feel. It's pure lightweight pop fodder yet oddly enjoyable, and the Icelandic grannies that Fálkinn targeted with the album will doubtless have loved it.

05 Jóhannes Kjarvalv

Few pre-teens would be moved to compose a flute-led semi-classical piece in tribute to a landscape painter, but such was Björk's approach on 'Jóhannes Kjarvalv'. Kjarvalv (1885–1972) worked in oils and celebrated Iceland's rugged, relentless natural beauty: he was particularly known for his studies of moss. Björk's homage to her much-lauded fellow countryman consists of a pensive, elegiac piano melody over which she winds an earnest yet evocative flute motif like a particularly precocious child at a school recital.

06 Fúsi Hreindyr

'Fúsi Hreindyr' or 'Fusi The Reindeer' is another Icelandic children's tale jazzed up and set to music by Björk and her musical helpers, and clearly betrays Fálkinn's wish to aim their child star's album at a Christmas market.

The track opens with sleigh bells, as all good Yule songs must, and then Björk sounds rather like pre-pubescent 1980s British choirboy Aled Jones as she sings the story of a reindeer who lives "in harmony with the waterfalls and the birdsong." A sax solo partway through the tune conjures ugly thoughts of jazzy prog-rock, but essentially this is a festive electro-doodle.

07 Himnaför

Translating roughly as 'Heavenbound' or 'Ascension To Heaven', 'Himnaför' is a surprisingly upbeat kiddie's bedtime song that opens like something by 1970s UK glam rockers Wizzard before Björk, sounding barely out of infant school, makes a breathless, somewhat shrill entrance. The tune, supported by handclaps and a sax solo, then bops along rather in the manner of the Jackson 5.

As sleep-inducing lullabies go, 'Himnaför' is somewhat unorthodox, proposing a lively nighttime visit to Venus, Mercury, Saturn, Neptune, Uranus and Pluto, before ending with a Mrs Mills-style piano solo, a volley of raucous applause and a throaty Björk chuckle.

08 Óliver

As well as Björk's fledgling offering, 1977 was also the year of Meat Loaf's rather more commercially significant album *Bat Out Of Hell*, and clearly Reykjavik had not escaped its influence. 'Óliver' opens with a hyperventilating, tumbling piano break not unlike that of 'You Took The Words Right Out Of My Mouth', but instead of Meat Loaf's stentorian howl, Björk's childlike tones then bob into view relating another ancient Icelandic folk tale.

'Óliver' sketches the Christ-like story of a beautiful boy in Valhalla who is nailed to a cross and receives the "rewards of victory" although his "hands are cold". A tragic tale, perhaps, yet the skittish musical arrangements and massed children's chorus are utterly at odds to any possible portentousness.

09 Álfur Út Úr Hól

Translating literally as something akin to 'Elf On A Hill', 'Álfur Út Úr Hól' is a cover of the Beatles' melancholic 'Fool On The Hill' from the *Magical Mystery Tour* album and genuinely affecting in the naturalistic strangeness of its interpretation. It's clear the pre-teen Björk was transported by the wide-eyed wonder of the Lennon/McCartney original and her swooping, hollering falsetto is the album's strongest vocal performance.

With gently mournful piano and ghostly flute lines, the arrangement of 'Álfur Út Úr Hól' is faithful yet imaginative, and as the track fades to a close, there is an early precursor of the unearthly, crystal-clear vocal for which Björk became so renowned a decade on.

10 Músastiginn

'Músastiginn', or 'Mouse Stairs', is the track on which Björk plays the smallest part on this first album, and one can surmise that this was probably the one which she was the least enthusiastic about. It's essentially a somewhat grisly Rick Wakeman-style mini-prog rock excursion for flute and guitar, interspersed with irritatingly flamboyant organ flourishes and half-baked noodling, and the *Dungeons & Dragons* musical mysticism reminds us that *Björk* was, in essence, recorded by a bunch of hippies.

11 Bænin

A mere two minutes in length, *Björk*'s closing track was 'Bænin' or 'The Prayer', a spartan little number on acoustic guitar which fittingly ends with Björk declaring "Dagurrin lidin, kommen er nott": "The day is over, the night has come." The pious lullaby appears to be loosely based on Melanie's 'Christopher Robin', depicting a small boy in hooded pyjamas on his knees giving bedtime thanks to God for "a good day". And is it imagination, or is the "Uss-hljott-hvad" whispering sequence in the chorus somewhat suggestive of the similar device in 'It's Oh So Quiet' a good two decades later?

Overall, Björk's childish enthusiasms and the muso competence of her collaborators lend this quirky album a certain ragged charm. It certainly appealed to her fellow Icelanders. The single 'Arabadrengurinn' became a chart and radio hit in Iceland, and the *Björk* vinyl-only album sold out its 5,000 pressing, earning it gold status in this relatively tiny music market.

Björk has always professed to be still fairly proud of her infant offering, although her positive feelings have never extended as far as actually allowing anybody to reissue it (Fálkinn are in no position to do so, having long ago transmuted into a bicycle manufacturer). There are also rumours that the master tapes have been lost or even destroyed. Consequently, original vinyl copies of this rarity can fetch as much as US$500, and there is an inevitable steady trade in bootleg CDs.

Fálkinn were delighted with the commercial success of their new child star, and offered Björk the chance to record a follow-up. The headstrong youngster had, however, already decided that there were side-effects to her newly discovered local fame that she was keen to avoid.

"I didn't want to make a second album when they asked me, because after the first one I got much more attention that I wanted before I was ready," she said.

"After I made my album, suddenly everybody loved it and wanted to be my friend and put me on the cover of magazines, and that didn't interest me at all. But it did help me sort out in my head very early on what my priority was – and that was music."

Björk's retirement at the age of 11 from the recorded music scene was to prove very temporary, however, even if there were to be no more

twee nursery rhyme albums. Björk was soon to be seduced by a new musical force whose tendrils extended even as far as Iceland. Punk rock was about to hit Reykjavik.

1980s

TAPPI TÍKARRASS, KUKL AND THE BIRTH OF THE SUGARCUBES

WITH HINDSIGHT, IT WAS ENTIRELY INEVITABLE THAT THE ANGER AND CONFRONTATION OF THE PUNK SCENE THAT BROKE OUT OF ENGLAND IN THE LATE 1970S WOULD FIND A WILLING DISCIPLE IN THE QUESTIONING, QUICK-MINDED YOUNG BJÖRK GUDMUNDSDÓTTIR.

"I think we hold the world record for how many punk bands there were for how many people lived in Iceland," she has recalled to English weekly music magazine the *New Musical Express*. "But it was very difficult to get English punk records."

These problems of access to the source didn't stop a crop-haired, shaven-eyebrowed Björk, who by now was 13, forming a definitively punkish all-girl quartet named Spit And Snot with three school friends. The furious foursome played a handful of bile-laden gigs around Reykjavik but, fortuitously, no music was committed to vinyl.

Probably tiring of thrash punk's rudimentary dynamic, Björk's next venture was a relatively experimental jazz-funk combo named Exodus, which allowed her to make rather more astute use of her musical education. Even here, though, it appears she chafed against the restrictions of a cerebral music that lacked the visceral passion she craved.

Björk was lucky, then, that a rare Exodus live gig was witnessed by a local musician named Eythor Arnalds, who was the guitarist in a punk/New Wave band named Tappi Tíkarrass – a name that translates, evocatively if somewhat indelicately, as "Cork The Bitch's Ass".

"My band played a gig with Exodus and we decided we had to steal Björk, which we did by persuading her that we were much more fun," Arnalds told Martin Aston in *Björkgraphy*. "Tappi Tíkarrass was a group based on friendship, fun, creativity and having picnics on the roof. We were different to the punks, though, because we almost looked like hippies."

They may have eschewed punk attire but Tappi Tíkarrass were well in tune with the envelope-pushing musical muse of the very early 1980s, being a surrealist, jagged, often wilfully pretentious affair. Lyrics were assembled via a William Burroughs-style cut-up, collage methodology and the music was melodic but intrinsically edgy.

Tappi Tíkarrass recorded a mini-album named *Bitid Fast Í Vitid* (or *Bite Hard In Your Mind*) and a full-length album named *Miranda*, both of which are virtually impossible to procure except on poor-quality bootlegs. They also contributed two tracks to a slightly higher-profile venture, a 1982 documentary and soundtrack album named *Rokk Í Reykjavík* (*Rock In Reykjavík*).

The *Rokk Í Reykjavík* movie depicted the city's thriving post-punk scene and showcased around twenty local bands. Both the film posters and the album sleeve carried an image of a 15-year-old Björk on stage with Tappi Tíkarrass, with large circles of rouge on her cheeks, an extremely severe haircut, and clad in a lurid yellow frock. She looked scarcely taller than the drum kit behind her.

Of the two Tappi tracks on *Rokk Í Reykjavík*, 'Hrollur' ('Shiver') opens over a routine plucked early 1980s bass line that could almost be Duran Duran, then Björk croons a sharp melody line before being joined by a male band member to bark sharp slogans. 'Dúkkulísur' is similar uptight white funk, whereon Björk sounds rather like Siouxsie Sioux of Siouxsie & The Banshees. Typically of those clipped, spartan post-punk days, both songs are over and done in less than three minutes.

Tappi Tíkarrass gained a certain local notoriety in Iceland until 1983, when Arnalds split the band in order to learn to play the cello. Björk claimed to be pleased by this decision: "I was just about to get bored with my band, because I had already tried everything I could do," she elucidated in *Björkgraphy*. However, she remained active on the local scene, even playing gigs with covers bands.

In late 1983, Björk was invited to appear on an Icelandic radio show by a local "alternative" DJ. Appearing alongside her were other musicians, including former members of Reykjavik scene stalwarts Purrkur Pillnikk and Peyr. They decided to form a new six-person band, Kukl (a rough translation is "Witchcraft").

"What was Kukl about? Basically we were terrified of mediocrity, materialism and a narrow-minded small town mentality," Björk has explained, thinking back. "That way of thinking was our enemy and we'd do anything to bring it down."

Kukl's musical director was guitarist Gulli Óttarson, who recorded under the somewhat presumptuous moniker of Godchrist. Björk, for her part, shared vocal duties with a spiky, abrasive and, above all, *shouty* local thinker and scenester called Einar Örn Benediktsson. They were to work together for almost a decade.

Kukl recorded two albums, 1984's *The Eye* and 1985's *Holidays In Europe (The Naughty Naught)*, that were both shot through with dark, brooding rhythms, an awkward and angular intensity and a sense of profound mischief. Due to their links with London-based anarcho-punk collective Crass, the band managed to record the albums in London and tour western Europe.

Kukl were not without a looming, adolescent air of pretension. A booklet included with the *The Eye* summarized the record's objectives, William Blake-style, as, "[To] depict The Marriage Of Heaven and Hell: The Union Of Opposites, Cold Claustrophobic Winters with the Agoric Midsummer Sun of the Summer Months …"

Looking back years later, however, Björk summarizes the ethos of Kukl in rather less lofty terms.

"It was basically about our very stupid local sense of humour," she has reflected. "We were a bunch of 16-year-old terrorists drinking absinthe we had smuggled from Spain and writing terrible tunes and being arrested a lot of times. We were just out to sabotage anything we thought was snotty."

Yet Kukl became the accepted voice of Iceland's new wave, criss-crossing Europe on tour with Crass and playing with The Fall, Chumbawumba and Einsturzende Neubauten. They continued to play when Björk was seven months pregnant by Thór Eldon, her boyfriend and fellow local Reykjavik musician. However, in 1985, due to the heavy drinking of some band members, Kukl split.

"I was crying for days," Björk confessed in *Björkgraphy*. "I was much more upset than I've been over any boyfriend."

The grief was to prove short-lived. Back in Reykjavik, Björk gave birth to her son Sindri on June 8, 1986 and also married Thór. Such domesticity didn't detract from the newlywed couple's creative urges, though. Together with ex-Kukl member Einar Örn, they founded a loose, subversive movement called Smekkleysa SM SF, or Bad Taste Ltd.

Essentially an ironic, post-modernist jape, Bad Taste instigated a Reykjavik arts awards show,

LEFT:
Björk with Sindri as a baby.

Tappi Tíkarrass,
Kukl and the Birth
of the Sugarcubes

19

ABOVE:
Sugarcubes live:
Björk and Einar.

formed a publishing company and staged "happenings" of varying levels of aesthetic worth. They didn't, however, have a musical wing, until they decided to form a band named Sykurmolar – or, in English, The Sugarcubes.

Comprising Björk and Einar on vocals (Einar also wielding a mean trumpet), Thór on guitar, Bragi Ólafsson on bass and former Kukl member

Siggi Baldursson on drums, The Sugarcubes played a handful of live gigs in Reykjavik before recording a debut single, "Birthday", that was nothing less than extraordinary.

Opening with a tilted, seductive bass rhythm and a muted trumpet seemingly played backwards, 'Birthday' transcended normal boundaries at the exact second that Björk opened her mouth. "She

ABOVE:
The Sugarcubes face the world.

lives in the house over there, has her world outside it," she breathed, seemingly rapt with wonderment. "Scrabbles in the earth with her fingers and her mouth – she's five years old ..."

Lyrically, 'Birthday' is the tale of an infant free spirit with "one friend/he lives next door", although Björk has implied the subject matter is rather less innocent: "It's a story about a love affair between a five-year-old girl and a man – it's his fiftieth birthday, but not many people can figure that out of the lyrics."

The song's true appeal, though, was Björk's alien, unearthly, scat-yodelling vocal performance on the chorus, which was genuinely like nothing that anyone had ever heard before. The track came to the attention of a sharp-eared British music press journalist, Chris Roberts, who made it Single

Tappi Tíkarrass, Kukl and the Birth of the Sugarcubes

21

Of The Week in weekly magazine *Melody Maker*.

Roberts' astute review led to huge media interest in The Sugarcubes. The group played London shows and became the subject of a major label A&R bidding war. "All of these companies came to Iceland and offered us fifty or sixty trillion billion pounds," Björk has explained, with her customary sense of under-statement. "We told them all to fuck off because we were still being terrorists."

The Sugarcubes did, indeed, resist the entreaties of their multi-national suitors and recorded their debut album for London-based independent label One Little Indian, for whom Björk still records (although they did sign a licensing deal with Warner Music for the US). *Life's Too Good* was released in April 1988.

01 Life's Too Good

The Sugarcubes' first album, *Life's Too Good* was a riot of freewheeling, spiky guitar pop which perfectly merged the band's punk and art-rock background with a vicious sense of fun and, tellingly, Björk's fast-developing otherworldly, insatiable vocal. It catapulted the group on to the world stage and set a musical benchmark that, in truth, the group were never again to equal.

The album opened with 'Traitor', a gothic reverie wherein Björk's somersaulting vocal plays second fiddle to Einar reciting po-faced verse about facing a firing squad. 'Motorcrash' is far more fun, Björk's forceful voice cutting through a galloping, hyperventilating beat to tell of witnessing a car accident that was "terribly bloody".

The tremulous 'Birthday' was the album's finest achievement, but 'Delicious Demon' was a further triumph, largely for the way the pure pop chorus works at angles to Einar's askew, absurdist poetry. 'Mama' was musically less defined but produces some memorable lyrical images, not least the big and pretty mother who is "drawing circles with her breasts in her jumper."

'Coldsweat' is one of the album's less striking tracks, being a turgid, brooding number reminiscent of the muddier moments of The Cure. By contrast, 'Blue Eyed Pop' is a sly, sarcastic pleasure, Björk and Einar hymning the delights of bubblegum over a halting, scratchy riff very suggestive of Pere Ubu.

'Deus' is second only to 'Birthday' on the album, finding Björk crooning whimsical, fantastical thoughts about the existence of a deity whom Einar, utterly deadpan, claims to have met: "He put me in a bathtub/Made me squeaky clean." 'Sick For Toys' sparked off a bouncy power-pop riff but was one Einar ludicrous poem too many, and finally 'Fucking In Rhythm And Sorrow' found a concerned Björk cheering up a naked depressive over, of all things, a rockabilly rhythm.

Utterly unlike any other pop record that had ever been made, *Life's Too Good* met with universal rave reviews and entered the UK charts at number 14. By the time the group closed their world tour – including their first ever trip to the US – in December 1988, they had sold 100,000 albums in Britain, and 450,000 in America.

Back in Reykjavik in early 1989, The Sugarcubes set about recording a follow-up to *Life's Too Good*. The group, though, were in a decidedly uncompromising, non-commercial frame of mind.

"When we became so famous and talked about after the first record, we said, 'Fuck the world' and decided to make the most unpredictable album we could," Björk told Martin Aston in *Björkgraphy*. "We all have in common that we are addicted to shocking ourselves."

The Sugarcubes succeeded in confounding all expectations with their second album, but few commentators felt this was a good thing. *Here Today, Tomorrow Next Week!*, when released in October 1989, received some of the most disappointed reviews afforded to a rock album for years. Where *Life's Too Good* sounded mercurial and alien, its successor appeared contrived and self-consciously zany.

The Sugarcubes had made a deliberate effort to return to their surrealist, contrary anarcho-punk roots, but too often the resulting album was merely irritating and, in a classic case of build 'em up and knock 'em down, the waiting media pounced.

02
Here Today, Tomorrow Next Week!

Here Today, Tomorrow Next Week! crystallized a feeling held by many that the rare, compelling beauty of Björk's voice was frequently subverted and destroyed in The Sugarcubes by Einar's self-regardingly wacky, grating interjections, and opening track 'Tidal Wave' only served to confirm this, as Örn shouted his trademark gibberish over his vocal partner and a semi-calypso rhythm.

'Regina' was far stronger, Björk's tilted and poised tones making the most of a killer chorus, but 'Speed Is The Key' was an annoying novelty piece over slap bass, and on 'Dream T.V.' Einar was once again what the *New Musical Express* summarized as "too damn pesky-menace-in-your-face." Then 'Nail' opened with Einar hawking up phlegm as if as a defiant symbol of the band's quest for ugliness.

'Pump' was one of *Here Today, Tomorrow Next Week!*'s few stand-out tracks, largely because Einar was for once relatively sidelined, giving Björk's voice space to soar. 'Eat The Menu',

though, was another painful lesson in Einar's school of the absurd ("Limousines, oranges, stars, moons, submarines...") and 'The Bee' was a negligible in-joke that should probably have stayed in the studio.

'Dear Plastic' found Björk declaring her love for man-made substances over a primal bass throb and erratic organ, while 'Shoot Him' had most listeners wishing to do this very thing to Einar ("I see my landlord/He is covered in gravy"). 'Water' is more compelling, Björk sketching a gorgeous word spell ("Hold your breath/And nestle into the ice") with Einar for once an effective counterpoint.

'A Day Called Zero' recalled 'Regina' with its edgy, stop-start dynamic allied to a bittersweet chorus, while 'Planet' for once dropped the superior, clever-clever vibe that polluted much of *Here Today, Tomorrow Next Week!* and allowed Björk to be engaged and enthralled by the world: "The universe is so big/I feel dizzy when I think about it/My head swims."

By 'Hey' we were back in pop vandalism mode, Einar gleefully trashing the song's shape as it begins to form, while the lairy 'Dark Disco' at least had the saving grace of perfectly reflecting its title. Finally, 'Hot Meat' was a reworking of 'Cold Sweat' from *Life's Too Good*, and found Einar adopting a "comedy" voice for his contributions. Few listeners could tell the difference.

The Sugarcubes were no longer media darlings and their sales suffered accordingly. *Here Today, Tomorrow Next Week!* performed poorly across the globe, selling less than a quarter as many copies as its predecessor. Furthermore, the group who had started out as a slapstick Icelandic art-rock joke found themselves subject to the usual inane, relentless pressures of pop stardom.

Björk needed some space and the chance to re-evaluate her musical direction outside of The Sugarcubes, and she was to find it in a project that could hardly have been more different from *Here Today, Tomorrow Next Week!*

1990

GLING-GLÓ AND THE DEATH OF THE SUGARCUBES

WHEN MUSICIANS TALK ABOUT "RETURNING TO THEIR ROOTS" THEY GENERALLY MEAN LITTLE MORE THAN RECORDING A BACK-TO-BASICS, FRILLS-FREE RECORD. IT'S TYPICAL OF BJÖRK GUDMUNDSDÓTTIR THAT SHE SHOULD INTERPRET THIS NORMALLY MEANINGLESS PHRASE INFINITELY MORE LITERALLY.

Returning to Reykjavik in 1990 after The Sugarcubes' world tour promoting the much-maligned *Here Today, Tomorrow Next Week!*, Björk decided to undertake a venture that had appealed to her ever since she'd sung in public with an Icelandic jazz group, the Trio Gudmandar Ingólfssonar, after the demise of Kukl. It was a project that the coffers of Bad Taste, groaning with funds from The Sugarcubes' global success, could afford to finance.

In just two days, Björk recorded an album of traditional Icelandic and jazz songs with the trio. It was to prove the perfect antidote to the pressurized, increasingly artificial vibe of The Sugarcubes.

"*Gling-Gló* was the opposite of The Sugarcubes' second album," she explained in *Björkgraphy*. "We'd fallen into the trap of spending two months on each song, whereas I have always been an obsessive fan of spontaneous music and behaviour. So I did that album in two days, which was so much fun."

The finished artefact, released in 1990 via Bad Taste, is a pleasing and successful exercise. Björk's idiosyncratic, maverick vocal talents frequently sound sublime set against the easy swing of pianist Gudmundar Ingólfsson, double bassist Thórdur Högnason and drummer Gudmundur Steingrimsson, who are exactly as accomplished as you'd expect a trio of sexagenarian jazz men to be. As an exercise in confounding expectations, *Gling-Gló* was nigh on perfect.

01 Gling-Gló

Named after the Icelandic children's phrase for a ringing bell – the English equivalent would be "Ding-dong" – Björk's venture into the world of scat and swing began with its title track.

Opening with sleigh bells played by Gudmundur Steingrimmson, the song soon shifts into nursery rhyme mode, Björk's preternaturally clear voice being entirely suited to such pat-a-cake rhythms. It's also fascinating to hear how her pitch and projection have developed since she last sang in Icelandic, on her eponymous childhood album.

Gudmundar Ingólfsson's fluid piano and Thórdur Högnason's erudite double bass gell sweetly as Björk trills a kiddie tale of Lasi from Leiti proposing to his lover Lina and being accepted beneath a moonlit sky. "The moon is special to lovers/Its light falls around them," the refrain runs, giving way only to a late funky bass run.

The expansive, spacious arrangement sounds fantastic, and it's hardly fanciful to hear the pleasure in Björk's voice that, for once, she wasn't compelled to share her creative space with Einar Örn's caterwauling and gale-force gibberish.

02 Luktar-Gvendur

Many of the songs on *Gling-Gló* are adapted from Icelandic sagas or folk tales, and it's soon evident that Björk's pitch and extraordinary flexibility make her ideally suited to such sumptuous story-telling material. She also forwarded persuasive reasons as to why such material is innately appealing to Icelanders.

"When Iceland was a colony for 700 years, ruled by the Danish, the people were all treated very badly," she's reflected. "They weren't allowed to dance or play music so we got obsessed with the sagas, which of course are very literature-based. The important music in Iceland is half-singing and half-chanting."

"Björk is a natural for traditional Icelandic songs," concurs Njáll Sigurdson, a Reykjavik folk music historian. "Her voice is neither a singing nor a speaking voice, but somewhere in-between."

'Luktar-Gvendur', or 'Gvendur The Lamp-lighter', is just such a ditty. Gvendur is an old man who walks the streets each night shining his light to enable people to walk in safety. A melancholic figure, his "damaged heart" will smile if he sees a courting couple, even if it brings back to him sad memories of his own lost love.

Thanks to a beautifully laid-back deep double bass groove, and some charming and sprightly piano from Gudmundar Ingólfsson, Björk is able to cut loose and abet the smokey jazz ambience with an impressively sensitive vocal performance.

03 Kata Rokkar

'Kata Rokkar' or 'Kata Rocks' is one of *Gling-Gló*'s more upbeat numbers, being a piano-led musical description of a firebrand named Kata, who "Full of charm and love of life/Knows so well how to rock." With "joy in her eye" the blonde-haired girl dances the rumba around a dance floor as happy admirers look on.

The song is lively but slight and Björk relishes the scope for lively interpretation, letting go toward the track's end with a series of delicious yelps and squeals. Her unorthodox technique is ideal for the demands of scat and she ends the song sounding as rapt and transported by music as is the mercurial Kata.

04 Pabbi Minn

'Pabbi Minn' or 'Oh Mein Papa' is an old Icelandic standard that had previously been a hit in the UK in 1953 for jazz trumpeter Eddie Calvert. It's a sparse, simple tune set to tinkling piano and finds the song's narrator paying homage to a loving father and happy childhood: "There was never anyone/As loving as you/Oh mein papa/You always knew me so well."

The undemanding vocal line is child's play to a singer as dextrous as Björk but she fulfils the song's rudimentary demands faithfully, tracking the chilled double bass diligently until the supper club number glides to a halt with a shiver of maracas.

05 Brestir Og Brak

Translating roughly as "Burst And Break", this lounge toe-tapper opens timidly and cautiously before leaping into the world of swing with a throbbing, insistent double bass motif and some carefully celebratory piano. Originally written by Jónas and Jón Múli Árnason, it's another traditional Icelandic tale rendered in textbook jazz club style, and Björk's stylings and phrasings are a delight throughout as she tackles the material with the relish and natural expression that is the hallmark of the entire album.

06 Ástartöfrar

Björk is well into Sarah Vaughan territory on this charming offering, a blue-tinged paean to the passions of the heart that translates as 'Lovespell'. Beautifully pitched and deeply resonant, her potent vocal cuts like a knife through the pliant double bass lope and skipping keys on what is a fairly conventional love song.

"I have often argued with Cupid/But never been hit so hard," she croons, rueing an infatuation beyond her control. "He aimed his arrows at me/And it was me who fell." Gudmundur Ingólfsson's smart, understated playing is a delight: clearly Björk chose well when she opted to work with the only professional jazz musician in Iceland!

07 Bella Símamær

'Bella Símamær' or 'Bella The Telephone Operator' is one of the sprightliest, most fun tracks on *Gling-Gló*, right from the sweeping, imposingly Beethoven-esque crashing piano chords that ironically, and misleadingly, open the tune.

The mood soon changes. 'Bella Símamær' is a musical portrait of a fun-loving, larger-than-life telephone switchboard operator who "knows something about everyone/tells you how long you've been on." "More fun and beautiful than any other," this Bella connects calls between lovers as her first priority, and flirts and jokes with her adoring customers.

Appropriately, the tune has a camp, celebratory, almost cartoon-like air. Strings prowl comically around a springy riff, and Björk bounces through the song with a chuckle in her voice, seemingly overcome with affection for this exemplary public service worker whose "eyes are blue and deep and bright/She smiles and laughs cheerily."

'Bella Símamær' has the gleeful charm of a kid's nursery rhyme – there are times it reminds you strongly of 'Nellie The Elephant' – but Björk's vivacious, lung-bursting enthusiasm is winningly contagious.

08 Litli Tónlistarmadurinn

With both lyrics and music credited, perplexingly, to

"12 September", 'Litli Tónlistarmadurinn' or 'The Little Musician' is a fast-paced, shuffling number whose hyperactive, rapid rhythms mirror the behaviour and speech patterns of the child who serves as the song's narrator.

Opening with sultry bass and busy maracas that lend the tune a Latin tinge, 'Litli Tónlistarmadurinn' finds an over-excited child climbing into its mother's bed in the early hours, declaiming "You are so sweet, my mama/I like coming closer to you."

The child – the gender is not clear – begins by stating grand musical plans for the future: "It would be fun to be grown-up/I'd conduct an orchestra and choir." However, the budding musician then gets distracted into relating the dream that s/he has just awoken from.

In the dream, the child's mother was a queen in a palace, lauded by all and entertained by a band of "elves and trolls". The mother/queen throws gifts to all of her suitors, but as the child catches one, s/he topples from its chair, simultaneously falling out of bed and awakening from the dream: "It upset me so."

A husky Björk relates this charming lyrical nonsense over forceful, intermittent piano and nervy percussion as the song shouts and trembles to a conclusion and the child gradually calms.

09 Pad Sést Ekki Sætari Mey

Björk's affection for show tunes is well-documented and her post-Kukl experience singing with covers bands had left her no stranger to the world of musicals, but this version of Rodgers & Hammerstein's 'There Is No Sweeter Girl' represents the first time she had committed such venerable material to vinyl.

The song is pretty standard musical fare, but Loftur Gudmundsson reworks some lyrics to add a little local flavour. "I discovered deceit when he spoke in his sleep/And I found out, he was very Icelandic after all," a tongue-in-cheek Björk muses, going on to speculate that the cad in question is "Just a poor Icelander/who wanted an Icelandic girl."

10 Bílavísur

Even by Björk's singular standards, 'Bílavísur' is a profoundly quirky affair. Set to a high-stepping, staccato beat, it finds the singer relating in breathless fashion the tale of a date in a car that goes disastrously wrong.

The tune opens with Björk in high spirits, excitedly accepting a telephone invitation from Dori, an admirer, to ride in his new car. "You're great, and very kind to invite me," she gushes. The enthusiasm is doubled when this "big and strong" Dori arrives in his "Ford Model Nineteen-Hundred-And-I-Don't-Know-What."

Björk steps inside and the duo set off on their

journey "to Mosfellstown" but the trip is ill-starred. Firstly, a loose spring in the passenger seat cuts her, then a "chain" breaks beneath the car, causing the hapless Dori to have to climb beneath.

Dori asks to borrow Björk's stockings to fix the car but succeeds only in ripping them, leaving her distraught: "I'll never go out with you again/I've never ridden in such a car". Finally the trip ends in disaster as a tyre bursts, the engine spits and roars and the vehicle careers into a mudpile.

Björk renders this picaresque curio with impressive flexibility, beginning the ditty cooing like a lovesick teenager and increasing in indignation as the date collapses around her. At the end the volume increases as she scolds and harangues the hapless Dori, climaxing with a disdainful growl and snort of disgust.

11 Tondeleyo

The Trio Gudmandar Ingólfssonar ease back on 'Tondeleyo' and leave space for one of Björk's most striking vocal performances on the whole of *Gling-Gló*.

Addressed to a "dark eyed" lover encountered on a trip to a tropical clime, the lyrical theme of 'Tondeleyo' strongly recalls 'Arabadrengurinn' from Björk's childhood album. Once again she meets a handsome stranger but this time, rather than mounting a dromedary, the pair bill and coo on a beach, then "drink, dance and kiss".

"Never were two hearts happier" Björk tells Tondeleyo, enunciating his name with awestruck longing, but the lovers are forced to part, and Björk exits the song regretting the fact that she was not able to see out her life "lying at your side in a native hut." "I have loved often since," she mourns, "but never as strongly."

Musically unremarkable, only Björk's yearning, cartwheeling vocal truly makes 'Tondeleyo' worthy of note.

12 Ég Veit El Hvad Skal Segja

'Ég Veit El Hvad Skal Segja' or 'I Don't Know What To Say' features lyrics by Loftur Gudmundsson, who also wrote the words to 'Bella Símamær' and 'Pad Sést Ekki Sætari Mey', and shares those songs' skittishness and lightness of touch.

This tune finds Björk in pleasantly bemused mode, pondering aloud the merits of three separate suitors who are clamouring for her attentions. "I ponder night and day/It's troublesome at times/To be as popular as I" she reflects, arguably more than a tad disingenuously.

Over a tumbling, piano-propelled beat, she considers tossing a coin to choose between her trio of would-be lovers but rejects this as impossible on logistical grounds. Clearly, though, a choice has to be made: "If I should choose to love all three, I'll end up all alone."

Thus resolved, she turns her attention to each boy individually. Jón "dances like an angel" but unfortunately also "drives like a fool" and, according to his mother, "snores like a ram/So I can't sleep a wink." Geir has different flaws: one night he suddenly kissed her then denied it, claiming "No, I bumped into you, that's all!"

"I think I love Svein," Björk ponders, turning her mind to the last contender, "but I never dare be alone with him." She's heard from other girls that he is a passionate and sultry lover but, as "a young and simple soul/I cannot say for myself."

Essentially a comedic mini-soap opera of a song, the playful 'Ég Veit El Hvad Skal Segja' comes over as an Icelandic take on 'Mama, He's Making Eyes At Me' but is, thankfully, far better than that comparison may suggest.

13
í Dansi Med Pér

'Í Dansi Med Pér' or 'Dance With Me' is set to the music of 'Sway (Quien Sera)', a Latin lounge tune penned in the 1950s by Spanish songwriter Pablo Beltran (or, as *Gling-Gló*'s sleeve wrongly states, Beltrani) Ruiz and lyricist Norman Gumbel.

Originally a hit in 1954 for Dean Martin, the tune has been intermittently covered over the years. Anita Kelsey sang a version on the soundtrack of Alex Proyas' film noir *Dark City* in 1998, and Shaft enjoyed a chart hit with a funked-up version they renamed 'Sway (Mucho Mambo)' during 1999.

Ruiz's salsa-friendly original was a sexy, sultry seduction, but on *Gling-Gló*, Björk turns it into a crisper, sharper creature entirely. Set against pert piano and precise double bass, she scats and yodels her way through the tune with a brisk efficiency that somewhat loses the intimacy of the original.

14
Börnin Vid Tjörnina

This folksy, cutesy little number opens with Björk playing a burst of mouth organ before tackling a song that is virtually acapella, with only a lazily plucked bass chord and spasmodic maracas interrupting her chirpy narrative.

Translating as 'Children At The Pond', 'Börnin Vid Tjörnina' is a traditional Icelandic children's song describing kiddies accompanying their father to a local park to watch ducks going "Quack-quack-quack". The infants feed the birds some bread, with the result that "Quack-quack-quack is full now."

Björk relates this somewhat mawkish material with an enthusiasm and energy that implies that another career could await her as a children's entertainer, should she ever require it. Her customary immaculate enunciation explains how the ducklings spend each night sleeping under the "blanket" of their mother's wing, and she explains that she once observed one of them lost and panicking on the water until safely reunited with its mother.

Despite this, the tune has a somewhat grisly conclusion. Winter arrives, the pond ices over, the ducklings are cold and sometimes "freeze and die". "The children mourn their quack-quack," Björk concludes firmly, "and so our story ends." Few adult listeners are likely to revisit it in a hurry.

15 Ruby Baby

The final two tracks on *Gling-Gló* are not just the only two that are sung in English but also date from a separate session that Björk recorded with Trio Gudmandar Ingólfssonar during August 1990, a month before the rest of the album.

'Ruby Baby' is a supple, be-bop classic written by legendary songwriting team Leiber (or, as the sleeve notes rather sloppily have it, Ceiber!) and Stoller, and over the years it has been covered by artists as various as the Beatles, Beach Boys, Gene Vincent, Dion, The Drifters, Donald Fagen and Link Wray.

Trio Gudmandar Ingólfssonar steer a fairly orthodox, mid-paced route through this supper-club standard but Björk treats this conventional arrangement as a launch pad for some truly stunning vocal acrobatics, pledging her devotion to the desired Ruby in a heartfelt tremor that could melt ice. It sounds tremendous, and not just because of its proximity to 'Börnin Vid Tjörnina'.

16 I Can't Help Loving That Man

The songs from the shows continue with *Gling-Gló*'s last track, a full-blooded and vivacious reading of a tune from Oscar Hammerstein II and Jerome Kern's 1927 musical *Showboat*.

Having a natural weakness for flamboyant, larger-than-life theatrical arrangements and declarations of pure passion, it's little surprise that Björk should go a bundle on this melodramatic pledge of eternal love. She delivers Hammerstein/Kern's ornery chorus "Fish gotta swim, birds gotta fly/I got to love one man til I die" with utter relish, and Trio Gudmandar Ingólfssonar's soft-shoe shuffle ease the vocal pyrotechnics – and the album – along to a satisfactory end.

Gling-Gló may be easily dismissed as a minor, left-field project for Björk, but this fails to take into view the nature of the Icelandic music market, where traditional songs are taken far more seriously than elsewhere. The album went platinum in its native land and made number 1 in the Icelandic chart.

Björk's next recorded project, however, was to be a far more high-pressure venture. The Sugarcubes were contracted to deliver one more album to their UK label, One Little Indian, and although Björk had extreme doubts about doing so, the band reconvened in New York in the summer of 1991.

Björk's misgivings were understandable. Far from the jovial, situationist pranksters of three years ago, The Sugarcubes had transformed into a mass of tricky tensions. Long since divorced from Thór, she also found her relationship with Einar had deteriorated. Her co-singer was tired of press reviews that stated, as he memorably told Martin Aston in *Björkgraphy*, "that I am a complete bastard who should be hung and quartered, and Björk is a sex goddess."

The more fundamental problem, however, was a diversifying of musical vision within the group. Björk had for months been growing increasingly seduced by the power and potency of house and dance music, regarding it as, "the only pop music that is truly modern." The Sugarcubes' voice-guitar-bass-drum format was beginning to bore her, no matter how whimsical their songs might be.

From these unpromising circumstances, it's surprising that The Sugarcubes' final album, *Stick Around For Joy*, wasn't a complete dud. Instead, the record, released in February 1992, has many stand-out moments, and was assuredly superior to the much-derided *Here Today, Tomorrow Next Week!*.

17 Stick Around For Joy

'Gold', the opening track on *Stick Around For Joy* was a halting, unsatisfactory affair that pulsed with the itchy semi-funk and self-conscious stop-start rhythms that were *de rigeur* on the British indie scene at the time. 'Gold' never really gets going and has few defining features except for Björk's striking vocal and a guest appearance by Public Image Limited-bassist and former Banshee John McGeoch.

The number that follows was rather different. 'Hit', appropriately, was the most successful single in The Sugarcubes' history. Over a funky, flavoursome bass riff, Björk delivered an account of falling deeply, unexpectedly in love: "This wasn't supposed to happen/I was happy by myself/ Accidentally you seduced me/I'm in love, again." Some critics speculated that the lyric described her new-found relationship with British musician Dominic Thrupp, or "Dom T". Maybe, maybe not, but either way this was an intelligent, resourceful pop song.

'Leash Called Love' was less immediate, being a circling examination of an abusive relationship. 'Lucky Night' opened with a typically Björkian lyric – "I've tried a lot, and most things excite me" – but then sagged under the weight of an unwanted Einar soliloquy delivered in a pained whine.

Despite this, *Stick Around For Joy* showed many signs that Einar's irritant role had been profoundly reined back, perhaps in subconscious reaction to the critics the band affected to despise. Often, as on 'Happy Nurse', he was permitted one terse interjection per song while no longer contesting the vocal spotlight with Björk – a contest, in truth, that he was always going to lose.

'I'm Hungry' debuted a theme that was to become a Björk staple in the year to come – one of fearless, experimental journeying into the unknown. "I wake up and know/That this is the day I'm leaving/I'm going alone/With no map/I need room, I need space ..." It's not fanciful to see the tune, further, as expressing her wish to leave the band that had begun as an adventure then turned into a cage.

'Walkabout' featured another busy, throbbing bass run as Björk fantasized aloud about running to hide in a beautiful landscape with a "delicious boy". 'Hetero Scum', despite being a song inspired by reading an article about radical homosexuals, is as near as The Sugarcubes ever got to dance music, as Thór and Bragi manage to get through a whole song without subverting its rhythmic pulse, a rarity indeed.

'Vitamin' was a hell-for-leather, clap-happy galloping anthem, and The Sugarcubes' recorded output terminated with 'Chihuahua', a moody and erratic number broken only by Björk's laughing rendition of the tune's title and Einar barking in the distance about aliens. It seemed as good a way to finish as any.

It had been evident during the recording of *Stick Around For Joy* that it was to be The Sugarcubes' last album. The band had drifted apart, and Björk explained her regrets, musical frustrations and need to move on in an interview with now-defunct UK weekly music magazine *Melody Maker*.

"We had known each other since we were nine. We loved and respected each other so much that

LEFT:
*The last days of
the Sugarcubes.*

it became difficult to assert your own viewpoint –
it was a bit like a marriage," she said. "We
became afraid of stepping on each other, which is
why I had to change partners."

The Sugarcubes bowed out by supporting U2
around the stadia of America, a tour that led Bono,
ever an astute judge of musical talent, to predict
great things ahead for Björk, wherever her musical
destiny might lead her.

"She has a voice like an ice-pick," he reflected.
"It seemed on that Sugarcubes tour that wherever
I was in the stadium, I could always hear her voice.
It could travel through metal, steel, concrete and
50,000 punters straight to my heart."

Björk's next musical venture would, in fact, be
very different from the askew, cunning guitar rock
of The Sugarcubes – and exactly how different was
about to become clear.

1993

DEBUT

THERE WERE NUMEROUS IRONIES ATTACHED TO BJÖRK'S RELEASE OF HER FIRST POST-SUGARCUBES ALBUM, *DEBUT*, IN 1993. THE MOST OBVIOUS, OF COURSE, WAS THAT THE ALBUM WASN'T HER SOLO DEBUT RECORD AT ALL: 1977'S ICELAND-ONLY RELEASE *BJÖRK* HAD ALREADY SEEN TO THAT.

The greater irony, though, was that at the age of 27, and having been involved in six full-length album projects, Björk Gudmundsdóttir was a long way from being a nervous musical innocent or virgin.

"I'd been making music for years," she's said, conceding the point. "I'd made music for theatre, film, pop stuff, jazz stuff, experimental stuff and electronic stuff. I must have worked with almost everybody in Iceland. I always had to work with other people's visions, though. Now it was time to write songs about me."

In truth, the genesis of *Debut* had begun long before the break-up of The Sugarcubes: in fact, even before that band recorded their swansong *Stick Around For Joy* album. Ever since 1989 Björk had been increasingly enamoured of the post-acid house worldwide dance scene and had frequently sought out experimental electronica, both in Reykjavik and as The Sugarcubes toured the world.

"I love dance music," she confessed to the *New Musical Express*, "because it's so fresh and new, so strong and romantic. Anything can happen. It's so innocent!"

In 1990, Björk had telephoned Graham Massey, a mainstay of Manchester acid house pioneers 808 State, shyly introducing herself only as "a musician from Iceland". She meet with the band, clicked, and ended up contributing vocals to 'Ooops' and 'Q-Mart', two tracks on their 1991 album *Ex:El*. She and Massey had also tentatively begun work on solo Björk material until the reconvened Sugarcubes intervened.

There was little doubt, then, that Björk's first solo post-Sugarcubes album would acknowledge the power and potency of cutting edge dance music. To recognize this fully, and facilitate the best album she was capable of, she realized she needed to immerse herself in a thriving, contemporary dance scene. Reykjavik was simply too remote, too far from the beaten track.

There was only really one place that offered her the riot of musical possibilities she desired and required: Björk decided to move to London.

"It was such a big decision to me to go to London," she has admitted. "Basically, I'm a really family-oriented person and the most patriotic Icelander in the world – I could be arrested for it! But London seemed like a melting pot for people from all over the world who were on similar missions to me, and somehow I knew that I was going to do an album of a kind that hadn't been done before."

Björk and Sindri moved in with her Belsize Park, north-London based boyfriend Dom T, whom she had by now been dating for eighteen months. It was Dom who was to introduce his lover to the man who was to become her major musical collaborator and partner in crime for the next three years – dance music producer Nellee Hooper.

Dom and Hooper were acquainted from both working as club DJs in their native Bristol a few years earlier. It was Hooper, though, whose star had risen the higher. Originally a DJ with local collective The Wild Bunch, he had moved to London to work with Jazzie B on Soul II Soul's epochal 1991 album *Club Classics Vol 1*.

"I didn't have any intention of finding a producer, I thought things would just happen by themselves," Björk told Martin Aston in *Björkgraphy*. "But Nellee and I started going out to clubs together, and after six months we were calling each other all the time with brilliant ideas, and it just took off."

Björk's initial plan had been for each track on the album to have a different producer, but her newfound closeness to, and understanding with, Hooper led her to revise that strategy. He admired her energy and constant fount of ideas; she was impressed by his production skills, studio know-how and sophisticated stylistic flourishes. The album was to be, as she confessed, "a musical affair between me and Nellee."

During the second half of 1992, the duo worked on the album, moving between a raft of London recording studios. Björk marvelled constantly as Hooper took her raw, fledgling song ideas and buffed them into a hard, brilliant sheen. They were a perfect musical team. Her weaknesses, she confessed, were "beats and overall sound" and Hooper was the acclaimed master of these particular areas.

In stark contrast to the machinations of The Sugarcubes, it soon became clear that rock music and guitars were not on Björk's musical agenda

ABOVE:
Björk joins Graham Massey and 808 State on stage at Manchester G-Mex.

this time around. Strings, electronica, harps and found noises were far more the order of the day. If her previous musical incarnation had ultimately proven restricting, this time around Björk was determined to be utterly adventurous.

Debut may have been a solo project, but still a string of musical partners beat a path to Björk and Hooper's door. Indian percussionist and tabla guru Talvin Singh was roped in, as was ex-Shamen vocalist Jhelisa Anderson and veteran drummer Bruce Smith from Mark Stewart's Bristol pop-punk visionaries The Pop Group. Octogenarian Chicago-based harpist Cocky Hale, whom Björk had first encountered on tour with The Sugarcubes in Los Angeles, was another partner-in-crime.

"I found myself attracted to people who knew as little as I did about what was going to happen," Björk reflected, years later. "Basically, I'm obsessed with people with exciting ideas. I've got no interest in working with people who do what I tell them to do – I need people who are as strong as me, or stronger."

Released in July 1993, *Debut* was an album that established Björk as a fascinating and entirely unique artist. Impossibly diverse, exotically eclectic yet somehow fluid and coherent, the album combined classical training, visceral poetry and the heady, insatiable rush of modern cutting-edge dance music into one integral whole. This was truly groundbreaking elegant, emotional electro-pop.

Yet while the influences were diverse and varied, there was no doubt that this album was all about Björk. For all its textural loveliness, this music was defined by her quite extraordinary, beguilingly alien vocal: her maverick vision and worldview held the myriad musical strands together. She had learnt from her collaborators yet not been shaped by them.

It was entirely appropriate, then, that the record appeared wrapped in a striking sleeve portrait of the singer by acclaimed French photographer Jean Baptiste Mondino. Clad in a baggy grey sweater, Björk faced the lens and the world with her hands delicately touching as if in prayer, a tiny diamond-like Indian bindi decoration beneath each eye. Singular, evocative and beautiful, the image mirrored the music that it contained.

Furthermore, compared to the deliberate punky primitivism of The Sugarcubes, this new project looked slick, streamlined and futuristic. Striking, stylized monochrome images filled the attractive CD booklet, and even the newly minted Björk logo, from the template of her signature, appeared a fitting design accoutrement to the impetuous, sheer music within.

Twenty-seven years in the making, this was Björk's *Debut* indeed.

RIGHT:
Nellee Hooper.

01
Human Behaviour

As soon as a clatter of sultry, dramatic timpani opened 'Human Behaviour', it was made clear to all-comers that Björk was laying down an aesthetic personal manifesto in complete contrast to the wayward, wilful mischief-making of The Sugarcubes. If anybody was expecting more surrealist odes to lobsters and God as a bathtub, this sleek, compelling new Björk would profoundly disappoint them.

The lush, opulent percussion that ushers in the track was in itself an early vindication of Björk's decision to draft in Nellee Hooper as *Debut*'s producer. Hooper had long been, due to his work with Soul II Soul, the acknowledged British master of elegant, panoramic soundscapes, and his luscious, pounding club rhythms were to prove a perfect platform for Björk's questing, querulous vocals.

It is, indeed, almost impossible to overstate the degree of separation and rupture between the angular arabesques and skewed irregularities of The Sugarcubes' perverse guitar art-rock and the sumptuous majesty of 'Human Behaviour'. The Sugarcubes' primary motive had always been art-shock confrontation and a sly, contrary nihilism. Björk, we were about to learn, was now playing by different rules entirely.

It is fatuous to ascribe the artistic leap made by Björk on *Debut* to mere production values; the differences are far more profoundly, personally philosophical and attitudinal. Nevertheless, it's clear from the first few seconds of 'Human Behaviour' exactly how much she was to gain by employing the studio suss and sensitivity of touch of Hooper. Compared to The Sugarcubes' often belligerent, scratchy production values, 'Human Behaviour' sounds lavish and lithe.

The track opens with a measured, humorously

self-aware rhythm which, together with a trademark Hooper funky drummer backbeat, marks out the song's musical parameters. Like most of *Debut*, the track builds on Hooper's knowledge of prevailing techno and house rhythms while giving Björk's vocal room to roam within an essentially stripped-back, sparse musical arrangement.

The beat, somehow sounding both camp and military (a military camp, perhaps?) beguiles, but Björk's flamboyant entrance truly enchants. "If you ever get close to a human, and human behaviour," she opens in crystal-clear, coquettish mode, "You'd better be ready to get confused." The lyrical message may be cautionary, but the delivery is fantastical. Freed from the sharing her vocal floor space with the wanton, vandalistic Einar, Björk had

never sounded so evocative or compelling.

Lyrically, the subject matter of 'Human Behaviour' is quintessential Björk, putting down a marker for the themes that were to recur regularly throughout her solo work. It's fitting that lazy critics routinely portray Björk as a kooky space alien from a different, distant realm, as she frequently contemplates her own, human species as though she is encountering them for the very first time, or falling to Earth like Bowie's Ziggy.

The alluring hypno-beat marks time like a funky metronome as Björk, the sensual anthropologist, continues her ingenuous dissection of her fellow beings: "There's definitely, definitely, definitely no logic to human behaviour/But they are so irresistible." The idea of there being "no map" to human peculiarities is a throwback to, and direct echo of, 'I'm Hungry' from the last Sugarcubes' album, *Stick Around For Joy*.

Björk may affect to stand a bemused, voyeuristic distance from her fellow man, but her feelings on the species are almost invariably positive, and she ends 'Human Behaviour' with a joyful affirmation: "To get involved in the exchange of human emotions/Is ever so, ever so satisfying." She may frequently raise her eyebrows at the vicissitudes of her cohorts, but ultimately she joins in – or initiates – the party.

'Human Behaviour' was a tremendous, highly appropriate introduction to Björk's solo work, and unsurprisingly formed the lead-off single from *Debut*. Released in June 1993, the song made little impact in the US, but sneaked into the British chart at number 36. As a mission statement for Björk's new musical mission, though, this rare and resourceful techno-hymn was nigh on perfect.

02 Crying

The lyrical theme of 'Human Behaviour', of feeling existential estrangement from your fellow creatures, alongside a deep, overwhelming love for them, was continued into *Debut*'s second track, 'Crying'.

Credited, like 'Human Behaviour', as a Björk/Hooper composition, 'Crying' adopts a more rueful, ruminative approach to human relationships. Over a busy, skipping bass loop, Björk observes herself perambulate around a metropolis: "I travel all around the city/Go in and out of locomotives/All alone …"

By pinpointing the moment in detail ("It's a hot day/And I'm dressed lightly"), Björk captures and amplifies the wonder she feels at her emotional dislocation from everybody around her who, like her, is innately "vulnerable". The chorus, though, makes clear her personal predicament: she's missing a faraway lover whose absence is making her ache ("Crying I can feel you").

'Crying' is one of the older songs on *Debut* which, Björk commented at the time, partly explained its more melancholic bent: the tracks written during the euphoric album sessions themselves tended to be far more upbeat in nature. Despite this, the trippy, quirky strings-and-synths backing to Björk's cascading vocal turns the track, inevitably, into another exuberant celebration.

At the end of the song, as Björk pleads for a ship to sail in, or an exciting stranger to knock at her door, her febrile vocal seems – and this, arguably, is her forte – to move beyond mere words and engage with the feel, the very texture of frustration. Against Hooper's deadpan, unshifting beat she sounds, as is intended, like a fearful,

riled lover beating her fists against a hard, unyielding fate.

03 Venus as a Boy

In many eyes the stand-out track from *Debut*, the rich, rapturous 'Venus As A Boy' found Björk throwing herself into a gossamer-delicate love song with typical élan and abandonment.

A solo Björk composition, rather than a collaboration with Hooper, 'Venus As A Boy' spirals open alongside a hopscotch, skipping beat and a ravishingly gentle string arrangement courtesy of Talvin Singh. Björk's love for show-stopping big tunes is once again evident here: this melodramatic romantic rumination could easily have come from the pen of George Gershwin or Cole Porter.

Except, of course, for the carefully erotic lyrics. Björk's habitual directness, plus the odd idiosyncrasy occasioned by writing in a second language, lead her into vaguely risqué territory: "His wicked sense of humour/Suggests exciting sex." Warming to the theme, she continues to render lasciviousness in the most poetic of terms: "His fingers focus on her/Touches, he's Venus as a boy."

In her enthusiastic, sometimes clumsily over-literal but eternally engaging way, Björk is always trying to define in words the very essence of desire, and 'Venus As A Boy' aches to locate such primal need: "He's exploring/the taste of her/Arousal/So accurate."

In most hands, any such attempt to render the act of cunnilingus in music would be utterly embarrassing, but Björk's headstrong determination to show it as simply one more act of love between adoring partners comes across as merely charming as does her repeated paean to her adored one: "He believes in beauty."

So who, if anybody, was the idyllic male praised so fulsomely in this magnificent music? Martin Aston conjectures in *Björkgraphy* that it was Dom T, Björk's lover at the time of *Debut*, but it's more tempting to regard the song as a glorious musical appreciation of anybody touched by the glow of love and open to adventuring and sexual experimentation.

"I love feminine boys with long, sensitive fingers," Björk has frequently confided to interviewers, and the delicacy of the intimacy described in 'Venus As A Boy' seems to entirely support this romantic preference. Beatific and languorous, this tune showed Björk at her most inventive, imaginative and immaculate, and reached number 29 in the UK singles chart when released in August 1993.

04 There's More to Life Than This

Few artists would follow a song as exquisite and drenched in beauty as 'Venus As A Boy' with a track recorded in the ladies toilet of a nightclub, but such was the setting for the riotous, demanding 'There's More To Life Than This'.

At Hooper's behest, Björk and her producer visited the loo at Covent Garden's now-closed Milk Bar to record this track in order to capture and communicate the sweaty immediacy and addictive buzz of the clubbing experience. Consequently the song opens with the chatter and hubbub of an early evening part-full club as the throbbing, insistent backing track is played over the Milk Bar's sound system.

Hand-held microphone in tow, Björk roams around the club, singing along to the streamlined techno pouring from the speakers around her. The lyric is an imprecation to a friend to escape an evening that is failing to fulfil expectations: "Come on girl, let's sneak out of this party/It's getting boring …"

"I'd gotten obsessed with making the album live, as opposed to some artificial studio experience," Björk explained, reflecting on the reasons for taking the tune to the Milk Bar. "This was the most true-to-reality song on the album because it reflected what me and Nellee had been doing between working on the album."

As the song progresses, Björk covertly slips away to the toilet, closing a cubicle door behind her with a very audible clunk, and drops her voice to a conspiratorial whisper as she contemplates alternatives to her current environ: "We could go down to the harbour/And jump between the boats/And see the sun come up." The plan deepens as she proposes that they "nick a boat" and "sneak off to this island."

Anybody familiar with land-locked London will know that such nocturnal maritime adventures are an utter impossibility, but the lyric to 'There's More To Life Than This' has its genesis in an evening Björk had spent in Reykjavik a few years previously when, true to the gist of the song, she met a female kindred spirit at a party and ran off to the harbour to drink and cavort with her new friend.

'There's More To Life Than This' is an engaging oddity, and anything but a novelty song. Despite the relatively inflexible techno beat (intended to convey the effect of a particularly flat, uninspired clubbing evening), this was another heady, experimental tune from a performer who was relishing finding her feet as a solo artist and giving expression to her remarkable, provocative lust for life.

05 Like Someone In Love

The divine, dreamy 'Like Someone In Love' formed the solitary cover version on *Debut*, being a cover of a rhapsodic jazz standard penned in the 1940s by Johnny Burke and Jimmy Van Heusen.

'Like Someone In Love' has enjoyed many metamorphoses over the years. Stan Getz, John Coltrane, Art Blakey, Sarah Vaughan and Oscar Peterson are among the jazz giants to bend it to

their wiles. Frank Sinatra turned the tune, as he did most things, into an effortless lounge croon, and pre-Björk it was also covered by artists as diverse as Perry Como, Jack Lemmon, Anthony Newley and Dame Kiri Te Kenawa.

Despite this imposing lineage, it's most likely that Björk became aware of 'Like Someone In Love' via an inspirational, landmark version of the track by legendary 1950s jazz trumpeter and crooner Chet Baker, a visionary and intuitive player whom she had once breathlessly described as "the most beautiful man in the world".

Björk's positively angelic rendition of the track is delivered acappella save for a gorgeous, succulent harp accompaniment courtesy of her Chicago-based friend Corky Hale. As with 'Venus As A Boy', Björk's task is to pinpoint the very feeling, the visceral ache and pang, of hopeless, headlong infatuation.

Nellee Hooper's masterful touch lends the song a grace and ethereality that is almost spooky,

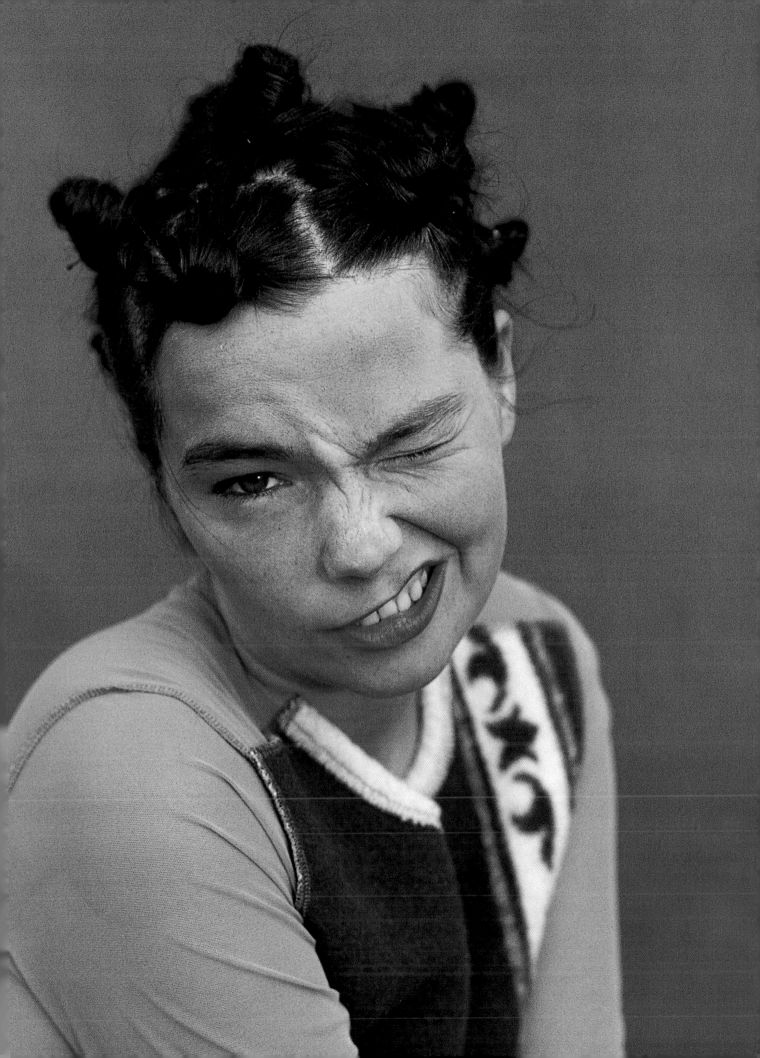

although interestingly this is the only song on *Debut* credited as a co-production (Björk was the sole producer on 'The Anchor Song', indicating that at this stage, she was far happier behind the mixing desk on slow numbers than uptempo club floor-fillers.)

As the song ends, a ravishing string section sweeps in to complement the harp and cascading waterfall effects as Björk does exactly what all great siren singers of love songs should do, and revels in the exquisite beauty of the moment.

The devoutly anti-retro, anti-conventional beauty Sugarcubes would surely never have permitted a cover version of this kind, and during this splendid swoon through 'Like Someone In Love' it may suddenly occur to the listener that the days of raucous, spiky interruptions by the rambunctious Einar Örn seem a long, long time ago.

06
Big Time Sensuality

Along with the opening track, 'Human Behaviour', 'Big Time Sensuality' represents probably the most compact and potent manifestation of Björk's new, post-Sugarcubes artistic manifesto on the whole of *Debut*. The drive and essence of this most singular of artistes is truly laid bare here.

Originally, 'Big Time Sensuality' was intended by Björk as a hymn of gratitude to her new-found ideal working partner and soul mate, Nellee Hooper. Around the time of the album's release, she paid typically effusive tribute to his talents and the expression his production techniques lent to her raw, unformed songs. Hooper, she made clear, had been exactly what she needed.

"With me and Nellee, it was very intimate," she admitted in *Björkgraphy*. "Even though I wrote all the songs, it's hard for me to take full credit for them because we were so dependent on each other. It was great – we even forgot about eating! We just got lost in music."

'Big Time Sensuality', then, starts off as a tribute to the creative chemistry that Björk immediately realized lay latent between them when she first met the Soul II Soul producer. Over an appropriately excited, hyperventilating club beat she itemizes her fascination with him, and with their potential: "I can sense it/Something important is about to happen/It's coming up."

Despite the specific nature of this lauding of her producer, though, it's equally feasible to read 'Big Time Sensuality' as a musical endorsement of one of Björk's philosophical hobbyhorses and interview exhortations. Miss Gudmundsdóttir has long been in the habit of insisting that the only life worth living is one lived to the full. Her existence, like her music, has never exactly been based on half-measures.

"I'm a very over-emotional person," she has frequently admitted. "I'm always very, very happy, or very, very sad, or very, very something else. I guess I just have a real Icelandic, Viking don't-feel-sorry-for-yourself attitude."

So as 'Big Time Sensuality' bounces and twitches into its huge, hedonistic chorus, it's impossible not to read the defiant sloganeering as Björk's personal *raison d'etre*: "It takes courage to enjoy it/The hardcore and the gentle/Big time sensuality." It's a pledge to all-round abandonment that reaches its euphoric peak in Björk's guttural, gleeful growl: "I don't know my future after this weekend/And I don't want to!"

The playful, explosive 'Big Time Sensuality' was released as the third single from *Debut* in November 1993 and, powered by a striking video showing Björk dancing on the back of a truck driving through New York City, reached number 17 in the UK chart. It also, two months later, scored Björk her first US hit when it made number 88 in the *Billboard* 100.

07 One Day

Although profoundly different musically, and a track which Björk wrote many months before beginning to record *Debut*, 'One Day' shares a lyrical philosophy with the preceding 'Big Time Sensuality'.

Björk, as we will note, has always returned to certain lyrical themes with an obsession that borders on compulsion. One of these is the thrill of anticipation, the unique emotional charge of awaiting imminent life-altering events; the sense, as she defined in 'Big Time Sensuality', that "something important/is about to happen."

'One Day' develops this theme of pregnant expectation of major developments, but the ambience is far more restful than the previous excursion. The mood here is gentle, pensive reverie and not nerve-jangling impatience. Björk is readied for some large development but, for once, she's laid-back about its arrival. Sooner or later, she knows the anticipated event is going to arrive.

Over baby gurgling and a swelling, lovely synth motif, she celebrates her preparedness. "One day it will happen/One day it will all come true." There are only two criteria waiting to be satisfied: the song's narrator must be "ready" and "up to it". The calm, circling percussion and electronica support this gentle sentiment like a hammock.

And what will happen when this blissful sense of readiness is reached? In one of the most beautiful stanzas on the whole of *Debut*, Björk elucidates: "An aeroplane will curve gracefully/Around the volcano/With the eruption that never lets you down." Not to mention, we should further note, "Two suns ready/To shine just for you."

Such evocative, perfectly crafted imagery hardly supports the somewhat limited view that Björk sometimes seem to hold of her own songwriting ability. "I'm neither an artist nor a poet, who can create something with words that can stand up on their own on paper," she told one interviewer around the time of *Debut*. "I can write a song in half an hour but it might take me four weeks to write the lyrics. It's not my natural way of expressing myself."

The longest track on *Debut*, 'One Day' is a masterpiece of mood, a spectacular summation of a feeling of bliss and belonging. Even the deliberately awkward line "The beautifullest [sic] fireworks are burning in the sky/Just for you," acquires well-stocked reservoirs of charm when voiced in Björk's heady, halting child-vocal.

08 Aeroplane

There is a case to be argued that every song on *Debut* is essentially about the state of desire and making such feelings of longing tangible, and 'Aeroplane' is yet another measured yet simultaneously impetuous Björk essay in insatiable yearning.

'Aeroplane' actually pre-dates the last Sugarcubes album. When Björk made her trip to Manchester to meet 808 State's Graham Massey, in 1990, she took with her a demo tape of the song played by Icelandic music students on just trombone, trumpet and two saxophones. She had asked Massey for advice on what to do with it next.

"It was just a quartet of brass instruments, and sounded nothing like what it ended up sounding like on *Debut*," Massey later recalled in Björk's 1995 book, *Post*. "You had to use a lot of projection and imagination to see what she was getting at by putting electronics in it."

If the melody to 'Aeroplane' was old, though, the subject matter was decidedly topical. While Björk was ensconced in London with Nellee Hooper recording *Debut*, her boyfriend Dom T was in Los Angeles fulfiling a lengthy DJing assignation. Despite the euphoria of the album sessions, the self-confessed "very over-emotional" singer missed her lover badly, and rewrote the lyrics to confront this sense of lack: "He's away, this ain't right/I'm alone."

Never afraid to be direct, in life or lyrics, Björk takes radical action to remedy her loss: "I'm taking an aeroplane/Across the world/To follow my heart." The mundane, pedestrian tabla beat that drags through the early song gives way to a brief, oddly comedic flourish of brass as she launches into the skies, and both the song and her feelings take wing.

Like 'Big Time Sensuality', though, the song's lyrical remit soon widens from a specific, personal Björk relationship to encompass the wider question of the very nature of desire itself. What, Björk basically asks, is love? How can such a free and independent spirit as herself be brought crashing down to lonely, needy dependency by an invisible force that is utterly beyond analysis? "How come/Out of all the people in the world/Only one/Can make me complete?"

Nellee Hooper provides the perfect atmospheric backdrop to such existential musings, dropping Talvin Singh's percussive shuffle on to troubled, parping brass and scattered found sounds as Björk muses aloud, beseeching the world for answers to her rueful rhetorical question. She is aware, though, there is only one solution: "One word on the phone/makes me happy/But one touch directly/Makes me ecstatic."

Low-key and understated, 'Aeroplane' is one of the less-celebrated pastel pleasures on *Debut* but is a mini-masterpiece of poignancy, regret and (temporarily) thwarted desire.

09 Come To Me

If 'Aeroplane' reflects the downside of love, the desperate, unbearable ache caused by being separated from a lover, then 'Come To Me' is its euphoric, blissed-out upside. Björk is back with her soul mate here, and staying put.

Björk songs often feel like an unstoppable outpouring of pure passion and primal emotions, and on 'Come To Me' the feelings are all utterly positive. Addressed to a close-at-hand partner, this soft-paced yet intensive eulogy is a pledge of support and unconditional love delivered over pulsing bass and twinkly, stardust electronica.

"Come to me/I'll take care of you/Protect you," urges Björk, addressing her beloved as though comforting a child. Indeed, the tone and language are so maternal that the song could easily be intended for her son, Sindri: "Calm down/You're exhausted/Come lie down/You don't have to explain/I'll understand."

Again, though, the specific person addressed in the song is less important than the overall tone of cocooning, cosseting infatuation. Björk's forte has always been the ability to maximize sensation, to inhabit the moment fully, and 'Come To Me' is a peerless exercise in voicing sheer, reckless devotion. Her love, indeed, knows no bounds: "Jump off/Your building's on fire/I'll catch you."

As absolute as love itself, 'Come To Me' is a many-splendoured thing, and as a romantic, velvet-hued violin sweeps across Talvin Singh's measured tabla tread and some elegiac electronica, Björk's tremulously intense vocal is truly compelling.

10 Violently Happy

"The unusual thing about her is how well she tackles joy," reflected U2 singer Bono at the end of the 1990s, contemplating Björk's maverick artistry. "Joy is the hardest thing of all to convey, whether you're a painter, filmmaker or rock singer. It's easy to paint with black and be angry. The ecstasy in Björk's voice is ... unusual."

It seems pretty certain that, in reaching that

conclusion, the Irish rock icon was musing aloud about 'Violently Happy', the most highly strung, vivacious, stimulated and genuinely euphoric track on the whole of *Debut*.

'Violently Happy' is a song of passionate, uninhibited extremes, and one inspired largely by the hedonistic clubbing evenings that Björk, Nellee Hooper and their various cohorts were enjoying during nights off from recording *Debut*. Interestingly, despite the mass categorizing of Björk's first solo offering as a "dance album" on its release, this is one of the very few tracks from it that a contemporary house club would even contemplate playing.

Nellee Hooper's background with The Wild Bunch, Massive Attack and Soul II Soul come triumphantly to the fore on 'Violently Happy', a souped-up, high adrenaline take on the bpm-frenzy acid house dance anthems that colonized the UK club scene in the early 1990s A burst of vigour and vitality, this is elegant, playful, superior dance pop *par excellence*.

Björk claimed in *Björkgraphy* that she wrote the track in autumn 1991, " ... about being stuck on an island and in love with someone on the other side of the planet." (as we know, a highly persistent Björk theme). As a consequence, 'Violently Happy' opens with more itchy, antsy feelings of dislocation:

"Since I met you/This small town hasn't got rooms/For my big feelings."

Yet where Björk's response to abandonment in 'Aeroplane' was morose, maudlin navel-gazing, here her reaction is very different. Adrift from her lover, she throws herself with full abandon into partying and celebration, interfacing with the moment, and denying any feelings of loss in one huge, all-encompassing embrace of life.

'Violently Happy' is a song about febrile, fertile, outlandish joy, an escape from the rigours and restrictions of routine that mirrors the altered state

LEFT:
"The ecstasy in Björk's voice ..."
– Bono.

enjoyed by legions of ecstasy-fuelled clubbers at the height of the acid house explosion. It's no surprise that the positivity and euphoria of that scene should have struck a chord with Björk, the puckish party animal who, laudably, never needs too much of an excuse to stick around for joy.

Nellee Hooper's nervy, elated techno-beats prove a perfect expansive platform for Björk as, casting around and seduced by endless possibility, she surrenders to the heady rush while still being aware that her impetuosity could lead to danger: "Come calm me down," she beseeches her absent lover, "before I get into trouble."

Björk's unique skill is to use her bizarrely expressive voice to convey emotions that are in flux, rapturous, beyond the reach of mere words, and 'Violently Happy' finds her almost bursting out of her skin with joy. Out of control, she is "driving my car too fast/with ecstatic music on', drunk and dangerous, she's 'daring people/to jump off roofs with me." Hooper's belligerent, urgent beats abet the sense of glorious excess throughout.

As the song – and the party – ends, Björk's still, submerged voice of calm recognizes that she needs comfort and comedown: "Soothe me" she pleads to her absent beau. Yet despite this nod toward the morning after, 'Violently Happy' is essentially a wild-eyed, evangelical endorsement of excess and adventure as everyday essentials: Björk, essentially, in a nutshell.

Released in March 1994 as the fourth and final single from *Debut*, 'Violently Happy' out-performed its three predecessors by charting at number 13, confirming that many of her more casual fans prefer Björk in clubby, dance-friendly mode.

11
The Anchor Song

It would be tempting to pigeonhole 'The Anchor Song', the sparse, echoing kiss-off to *Debut*, as the comedown after the impossible dementia of 'Violently Happy', were it not for the fact that this spartan, sensual track exudes its own self-contained beauty.

Inspired by a solo cycling jaunt around Iceland, and written on a church organ, 'The Anchor Song' stands apart from the majority of the eclectic, multi-cultural tracks on *Debut* in being quite obviously inspired by Iceland and, in particular, the harbour in Reykjavik to which Björk ran with her nocturnal friend in 'There's More To Life Than This'. Björk originally played a rudimentary debut of this track to 808 State's Graham Massey in 1990, when she also debuted 'Aeroplane'.

Björk gave Nellee Hooper the night off when she came to record 'The Anchor Song', evidently feeling confident that even her embryonic production skills could handle the track's rudimentary instrumentation and arrangements. She was joined on the track by English saxophonist Gary Barnacle, who had previously played on 'Tidal Wave' on The Sugarcubes' second album *Here Today, Tomorrow Next Week!*. Oliver Lake, of Björk faves the World Saxophone Quartet, later reshaped and re-jigged the sax parts on the song.

The wild, blasted landscape of Iceland and, in particular, the ocean are perennial Björk lyrical staples. Even during the head rush of 'Violently Happy', she had found time to "tip-toe down to the shore" and make the ocean "roar" at her. 'The Anchor Song' finds her in mellower mood as she contemplates her maritime setting.

"I live by the ocean," she trills, over a grave accompanying brass section, "and during the night/I dive into it." Like a night swimmer, her breathing is deep and regular. Gary Barnacle's sonorous sax punctuates her every utterance, giving her time to take in air. Engagingly, 'The Anchor Song' appears to develop before us in slow motion.

As the heavy, careful brass blows around her, Björk continues her descent beneath the waves to the bottom, where she drops anchor. Finally, acappella and with a voice trembling like a night air shiver, she defiantly embraces the womb-like

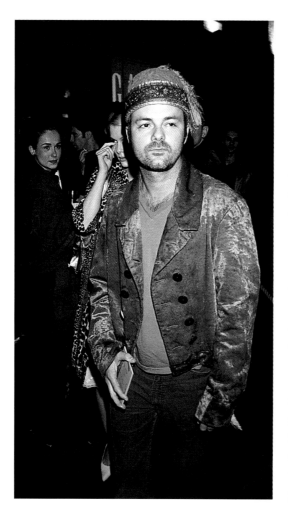

depths: "This is where I'm staying/This is my home." The rest is silence, save for Barnacle's sax repeating its motif like a mournful last post.

Björk dismissed 'The Anchor Song' in *Björkgraphy* as "a very simple song with silly lyrics." More likely, though, it's a natural progression for an artist who, only three years previously, had recorded an album of traditional Icelandic songs and fairy tales and who boasts of being "so patriotic that [she] could be arrested." Despite her move to cosmopolitan London, the closing track's subtext ran, Björk remained a creature of Iceland.

"I never go out of my way to be Icelandic," she reflected at the time, questioned on the song's provenance. "Iceland is just so subconsciously in me that I don't need to focus on it consciously as well."

As the closing track on *Debut*, 'The Anchor Song' also served notice on any casual dance fans seduced by 'Violently Happy' or 'Big Time Sensuality' that Björk was anything but one more interchangeable club diva. As numerous press reviews and gobsmacked journalists queued to announce, a major new star had arrived.

Debut was released in July 1993 to a media fanfare, but probably the most accurate review of this startling, envelope-pushing "new" talent came from Björk's closest confidante and fellow plotter during the making of the album, Nellee Hooper.

"I must have listened to each of these tracks more than 500 times since we started," Hooper wrote on the sleeve notes to *Debut*. "Everything's long since finished but I'm still listening to these songs every day. I'm wondering ... will this ever stop? We are so lucky to have Björk's voice!"

One Little Indian managing director, Derek Birkett, Björk's long-time friend and co-manager, had serious misgivings about the direction of her solo project but indulged his protégée, telling her he believed it would probably sell around one-third of the figure usually reached by Sugarcubes albums. The indie impresario has surely never been so pleased to be wrong.

Critical approval for *Debut* was nigh on unanimous, with London listings magazine *Time Out* taking the garland for hyperbolic enthusiasm by describing it as "the most original, musical music to come out of the dance-pop *milieu* since the disinvention of the human bassist ... the most complete pop music of the decade." Bizarrely, Simply Red's Mick Hucknall compared Björk to Billie Holiday and requested the chance to do a remix (this was granted, on a single version of 'Venus As A Boy').

With reviews and word-of-mouth on *Debut* looking fantastic, Björk set about assembling a band to tour the album. The personnel were mixed and varied. Talvin Singh ventured out on the road with her, as did programmer Guy Sigsworth, keyboardist Leila Arab, multi-instrumentalist Dan

Lipman, bassist Ike Leo and drummer Tansay Omar. Björk, it seemed, was relating to people who, like her, were displaced from their home environment.

"I didn't plan it," she reflected, "but I ended up with a band that was one person from Iran, one from India, one from Turkey, one from Cyprus and one from Barbados. We were like Immigrants United!"

Björk was spending a lot of time hanging out in Hounslow, west London, investigating bhangra and Bollywood soundtracks, so was happy to announce to mildly bemused journalists that her live revue was essentially "an Indian disco pop band". She took this singular ensemble around the UK and Europe then, as 1994 dawned, continued to Australia and Japan.

As Björk traversed the globe, *Debut* continued to sell and sell. The eccentric, wilfully eclectic project by a single-minded chanteuse that even her manager thought would struggle to sell 100,000 copies suddenly became an accoutrement to every coffee table around the globe. Suddenly, *Debut* had gone platinum in the UK, peaking at number 3, and gold in America, where it reached 61 in the *Billboard* chart.

This extraordinary success was recognized at the British music industry's prestigious BRIT Awards, where Björk was named Best International Female Artist and Best International Newcomer. She celebrated with a show-stealing duet with Polly Harvey of PJ Harvey fame and their intensive, demanding cover of '(I Can't Get No) Satisfaction' by the Rolling Stones guaranteed that even more attention would be coming Björk's way.

One contrary, underground star had suddenly gone decidedly overground.

LEFT:
Björk with Polly Harvey.

1994

POST

As 1994 progressed, Björk continued her world tour and released a remix album, *All The Remixes From The Same Album For Those People Who Don't Buy White Labels*. She may by now have been a major international star, but the title confirmed that the mischievous, anarchic sense of humour that had powered The Sugarcubes was still intact.

Björk reinforced her reputation as a free spirit by declining an invitation from Madonna to co-write the American's new album, together with Nellee Hooper. She did write 'Bedtime Story' for the megastar, who gratefully made it the centrepiece of her *Bedtime Stories* album even after Björk rebuffed her invitation to make the song a duet, telling *Rolling Stone* "my intuition told me that it would be wrong."

Nonetheless, the very fact that the invitation had even been extended by the world's biggest pop star showed that Björk was now working under very different rules from those that affected the unknown star from cult band The Sugarcubes recording her first solo album two years earlier. When Björk set about recording the follow-up to *Debut* in late 1994, she knew she had a tough job on her hands.

"I think one of the reasons *Debut* is the way I wanted it to be is because I could do it in my own corner without anyone poking at me," she reflected in *Björkgraphy*. "I'm probably not going to get the same peace next time around unless I do it totally on my own and don't let anybody hear it for a year."

Compared with her solo endeavours post-Sugarcubes, Björk began work on her second album at the very end of 1994 with an absolute army of helpers. Graham Massey of 808 State was involved with pre-production, and the pair revisited some song ideas they had worked on pre-*Debut*. DJ and producer Howie Bernstein, aka Howie B, a rising star who had engineered on *Debut*, also came to the fore.

Björk was understandably keen to revive the partnership with Nellee Hooper that had yielded such spectacular results on *Debut*, but found Hooper – who, by now, had agreed to produce Madonna's *Bedtime Stories* – less enthused than previously. The duo eventually agreed that Hooper would oversee the project while not being as inextricably involved as he had been on *Debut*.

Hooper was keen to capture a back-to-nature vibe on Björk's second album by conducting much of the recording outdoors, a suggestion with which the singer heartily concurred. He originally suggested recording at a hilltop studio in Capri, Italy, but this was vetoed on grounds of the winter weather, although Björk was eventually to record her third studio album, *Homogenic*, in a similar southern European location.

So, an alternative decision was taken: Björk was going to the Bahamas.

In early 1994, Björk flew out to Compass Point studios, Nassau, with Nellee Hooper plus Howie B and Marius De Vries, Hooper's first-choice engineer who had also worked on *Debut*. Team Björk set about a series of highly unusual and intensive recording sessions that were, eventually, to yield the album that became *Post*.

Phil Spector would certainly have baulked at the unorthodox recording techniques that went into the record. Firstly, Björk recorded most of her vocals on the beach. Clutching a tiny hand-held microphone, she would wander into the ocean or across the lush Caribbean landscape committing her voice to tape. On a primal level, it was exactly what she craved.

"I'd go running into the water and nobody could see where I went," Björk recounted to *Interview* magazine. "In the quiet bits I'd sit and cuddle and for the outrageous bits I'd run around. It was the first time I'd done a song like that in twenty years and I was crying my eyes out with joy because it was something I so deeply wanted all those years."

But what exactly was Björk recording out there? Many artists suffer from the much-documented "Second Album Syndrome": having had, in most cases, two decades to dream up material for their first record, they suddenly find they have to find songs for its follow-up in a matter of weeks. Björk didn't seem to suffer from this pressure, possibly because of her rather singular personal mental filing system.

"I do most of my creative work in my head while I'm doing other things," she has explained. "I've got very organized in my head. I've got all these

little sections, like cupboards and drawers, and I can put ideas in a cupboard in my head and come back to it a year later and it will still be there. So I might look as if I'm just starting a song, but really I've been working on it for a year."

The sessions in Nassau were seemingly idyllic, an impression reinforced by photos of Björk roaming through beach caves and cuddling with Marius and Howie B in the lush, sumptuous *Post* book (Bloomsbury, 1995), which Björk produced to explain the album's making and serve as a tour programme on the subsequent world tour. Björk and Nellee appeared to have succeeded in their aim of making the record more organic and less computer-driven than its successor.

Nevertheless, when the party returned to London, Björk experienced a crisis of confidence and immediately insisted on a lengthy process of re-recording which few, if any, of her colleagues truly believed was justified.

"Björk tends to pull things to pieces," Marius De Vries confided in Martin Aston in *Björkgraphy*. "She has extreme reactions to things, which is a virtue as well as a fault."

Nevertheless, a few feverish re-recording sessions later, Björk finally deemed *Post* ready to face the world. Thanks to the involvement of Graham Massey, plus her own greater confidence behind the mixing desk, only four tracks out of eleven were eventually given joint co-producer credits between Björk and Nellee Hooper. Nellee was still heavily involved, but clearly he was no longer Björk's sonic mastermind.

Post finally appeared, in June 1995, tellingly wrapped in a far more lustrous cover than the fairly minimalist portrait of *Debut*. In a shot taken by Stephane Sednaoui, who had been her lover since he shot her full-length video *Vessel*, Björk stared out from a cover rich in lush pinks and purples, clad in what appeared to be an air-mail envelope. Oriental letters and a parasol played up her distinctly Eastern-looking features.

Sednaoui was a second choice; Björk originally commissioned, then scrapped, an album cover shoot with Jean Baptiste Mondino, who had created the *Debut* sleeve. Nevertheless, the image was striking and instant and, from the first track onward, served to complement the expressive nature of the music within. Her legion of helpers had, it was clear, helped her to craft a highly distinctive and varied record.

"I've become better at what I am doing," Björk explained, with engaging simplicity. "In a way, *Debut* and *Post* are the same thing – but the before and after. The first one was done while I was still a virgin, musically; the second one when I knew a little bit more."

01 Army of Me

With its cavalcade of menacing, punishing machine-rhythms and threatening, no-nonsense lyrical bent, 'Army Of Me' was a surprising and extremely atypical opening to Björk's eagerly anticipated second album. So was this what she had been up to?

A riot of sinister, troubling beats, the song had its origin in Björk's solo sessions with Graham Massey before she began work on *Debut* with Nellee Hooper. The duo had sat down and written the bare bones of both this track and 'The Modern Things' in a single afternoon in 1992. "We just sat there and giggled," recalled Björk in her *Post* book.

'Army Of Me' found Björk in the most defiantly independent of moods. Over the suitably uncompromising quasi-industrial beat, she mirrors the harsh, disciplinarian ambience by demanding that the hapless soul she is addressing shows a little self-control: "Stand up, you've got to manage/I won't sympathize, anymore."

Björk's ice-cool, innately pure vocal is a thrilling contrast to the sinister, military pulse of the song, which quickens and deepens as she sparks into the chorus: "If you complain once more/You'll meet an army of me." Together with the later demand for "self-sufficience" [sic], the song functions as a decidedly anti-liberal demand for any weak-willed slackers to stop moaning and pull themselves together.

"It's me saying, 'Just get to work, stop this, please,'" Björk told British music mag *Melody Maker*. "You come to a point with people like that where you've done everything you can do for them, and the only thing that's going to sort them out is themselves. It's time to get things done."

It's not hard to imagine the fiercely independent Icelandic single mother who, at the age of 27, left her homeland and family to pursue her career single-mindedly holding such views, but nonetheless 'Army Of Me' was an unexpectedly strident return for many fans expecting more of the life-affirming and/or serene pleasures of *Debut*.

Possibly for that very provocative reason, and against the advice of her long-suffering manager and label boss Derek Birkett, 'Army Of Me' was released in April 1995 as the first single from *Debut*. It reached Björk's highest UK chart position to date of No 10, partly powered by a TV appearance backed by metal-leaning labelmates Skunk Anansie, who were fronted by charismatic shaven-headed female singer Skin.

"I do a metal thing on Top Of The Pops, which I thought was quite shocking," Björk laughed to *Q* magazine later, "and most people just go, 'Oh yes'. I've lost the plot, to be honest. Not that I ever had it."

'Army Of Me' also appeared on the soundtrack to the blockbuster movie *Tank Girl*, which was released shortly after the single and starred Lori Petty as a warrior-babe fighting the good fight against evil water-hoarding authorities in a drought-ridden 2033. Björk's song was widely considered, by most observers, to be the best thing about the fairly cliché-ridden, routine adventure movie.

02 Hyper-Ballad

After the strident and discordant opening of 'Army Of Me', 'Hyper-ballad' was a more reassuring second track for any recent fans, seduced by *Debut*, who were looking to *Post* for more quintessentially, typically Björkian pleasures.

The album's first Björk/Nellee Hooper co-production, 'Hyper-ballad' once again benefits from the Soul II Soul man's rare stylistic grasp of dance dynamics. Over a lush, sunrise synth and crafty percussion, Björk relates a seductive tableau in her trademark wondrous croon. As a splendid poetic essay romanticizing the everyday, it's an evocative triumph.

In the *Post* book that accompanied the album's release, Björk spoke of the track as inspired largely by the savage, extreme realities of Iceland. "It's the survival of the fittest, it really is," she said. "We are born to exaggerate and do the maximum."

'Hyper-ballad', though (and its odd staccato sentimentality is very true to its title) makes more sense seen as another Björk hymn to the moment, an existential howl of joy at the human condition combined with the calm satisfaction that accompanies being safely ensconced in a loving relationship. It's this mix of danger and domesticity that, as ever, is her strong suit.

Björk relates how each morning, as her partner sleeps, she sneaks out to throw rocks off cliffs and feel alive while also, paradoxically, visualizing her own death: "I imagine what my body would sound like/Slamming against those rocks." Her voice sounds tremendous, tremulous, and the points of detail are exquisite: as she falls to her

death, she wonders, will her eyes be closed in fear or fixed wide open?

As Björk's wonderings grow wilder and fiercer, Nellee Hooper ups the musical tempo until she is singing over a pummelling techno beat, catching her breath, seemingly frightened for her life. Yet still she returns, purged and grateful, to the arms of her unaware, sleeping lover, "Happier to be safe again with you."

'Hyper-ballad' ends, after the dancefloor-friendly tumult, with some gorgeously luscious strings orchestrated by Eumir Deodato, a veteran Brazilian modern classical composer whose work Björk had long admired. It's a fine piece of work and, when released as the fourth single off *Post* in February 1996, reached number 8 in the UK.

03
The Modern Things

'The Modern Things' was the second of the two tracks dreamed up by Björk and Graham Massey on that giggly afternoon in Manchester in 1992. Björk, in fact, goes so far as to claim that she composed the bare bones of the song on the Inter-City train from London on the morning of their meeting.

Musically, 'The Modern Things',

a Björk/Massey/Hooper co-production, has far more in common with the halting, angular 'Army Of Me' than the tumbling, vivacious 'Hyper-ballad'. Across a Marius De Vries-programmed busy, irregular rhythm, Björk relates a clever-stupid child's fable that claims that modern electronic / mechanical devices ("like cars, and such") have patiently concealed themselves inside mountains since the day of the dinosaur ("for the right moment").

Specifically, the song was aimed at people whom Björk regarded as hapless Luddites unable to cope with progress and modernity. Some critics, for example, had lambasted her abandoning the "authentic" indie-leaning guitar rock of The Sugarcubes for experimental electronica.

"What is the difference between using electricity and electronics as tools, or stroking strings and wood?" she demanded of one accuser. "I find it amazing when people tell me that electronic music has no soul and blame the computers! If there's no soul in the music, it's because somebody forgot to put it there."

So, in a prolonged analogy that possibly gave fuel to those observers who claim that Björk can be irritatingly whimsical and clumsily over-literal, 'The Modern Things' finds her developing the analogy until the contemporary objects emerge from their subterranean lair "To multiply and take over/It's their turn now." The song ends with Björk's gentle, undeniably precious vocal repeating on a loop until snapped off, like a stuck needle being lifted from a vinyl record.

04
It's Oh So Quiet

Vibrant, vivacious and gloriously burlesque, the show-stopping 'It's Oh So Quiet' was the song that finally lifted Björk from significant cult status to being a major league star and, at least in her adopted Britain, led tabloid newspapers and the more prurient media in general to begin to focus their gaze upon her. It was also a highly fitting tune for a gal who, let us not forget, could sing the whole of *The Sound Of Music* at the age of three.

The sole cover version on *Post*, this melodramatic opus developed Björk's tradition of covering meta-romantic old standards such as 'I Can't Help Loving That Man' on *Gling-Gló* and, of course, 'Like Someone In Love' from *Debut*. For sheer larger-than-life, lung-bursting élan, though, this was the daddy of them all.

'It's Oh So Quiet' was originally written by songwriting duo Hans Lang and Bert Reisfeld for Hollywood starlet Betty Hutton, who sang it in 1948. After Björk turned the song into a hit, Hutton's label made the original version available again, along with tracks like 'Who Kicked The Light Plug?' ('It's Oh So Quiet' was originally called 'Blow A Fuse') on a cash-in greatest hits album, *Betty Hutton: The Best Of The RCA Years*.

Björk was first played the Hutton original by her sometime musical collaborator Guy Sigsworth, and found herself deeply enamoured of it, declaring to *Details* magazine in the US that it was "the best song in five years." She was determined to cover the tune, even though it was "against my principles to do an old cover version because I'm so anti-retro."

If a "cover version", though, implies a fairly tired, routine trudge through the motions, Björk's full-on assault on 'It's Oh So Quiet' was anything but. Gaining from a superlative Nellee Hooper co-production, she made the tune entirely her own, infecting it with a vibrancy, passion and humour that were genuinely breathtaking. The supposed cult star, it rapidly became clear, could mix it in the commercial arena with the best of them.

Lang and Reisfeld's riotous original was intended as a hilariously overblown, joyous celebration /parody of the intoxication and dementia of extreme love, and Björk ensured that none of the hyperbolic hysteria was lost in the mix. The song's comic dynamic demanded a restrained, understated opening as its protagonist reflected her inner peace, and Björk sounds positively demure …

… until the chorus kicks in. Björk's miraculous vocal prowess is immaculately suited to the yelped histrionics of the delirious, garrulous lover, and she clearly relishes the high drama of the tumultuous "zing, boom!" sequence as Nellee Hooper lights the production blue touchpaper around her. This was a torch song as in truly aflame. Björk had made her name via subtler pleasures, sure, but this flamboyant number was certainly big fun.

Björk and Nellee Hooper repeat the quiet-loud peace-passion trick twice more as the song demands, Björk particularly rendering the lines "You blow a fuse/The devil cuts loose" with extraordinary expressiveness. It's easy to see why this half-a-century-old tune appeals to her so greatly: in spirit, the lyric is little removed from the ingenuous, exhilarated wonder of her own 'Aeroplane' on *Debut*, a rather more muted but equally marvelling paean to the power of love.

The song's extravagant camp and comedic, cute "Ssssh!" whispering sequences made the number a natural single, even if it was a "retro cover". 'It's Oh So Quiet' was released in Britain in November and set off on an inexorable climb up the chart. Powered on its way by a suitably over the top 1940's all-singing, all-dancing video by Spike Jonze, 'It's Oh So Quiet' even flirted with the notion of being a Christmas number 1 before eventually peaking at number 4, behind Michael Jackson's 'Earth Song'.

Sadly, although this rousing roustabout of a song introduced Björk to a far wider audience, its success had a sting in the tale. Soon tiring of its ubiquity, as do many artists who see one, often atypical song become far more popular than the rest of their *oeuvre* (cf. Radiohead, when they were known as "The 'Creep' Band"), Björk eventually publicly regretted covering 'It's Oh So Quiet' and has not played it live for many years. Probably, she never will again.

05 Enjoy

It is difficult to envisage a greater songwriting contrast between 'It's Oh So Quiet' and the track that follows it on *Post*, the turbulent, dark-edged 'Enjoy', written by Björk with – and about – her sometime lover Tricky.

Just as Björk was beginning pre-production on *Post*, in late 1994, she was also ending her love affair with French photographer Stèphane Sednaoui, even though he was still to supply the album's cover image. His romantic replacement, though, was to raise many eyebrows in the music world.

Through Nellee Hooper, Howie B and their Massive Attack/Bristol connections, Björk had been introduced to Tricky, the artful, stoner poet-rapper who had contributed to both Massive albums to date, *Blue Lines* and *Protection*. Tricky

electro-riff fights for space with Björk's pensive, dawdling organ as the track opens, creating an unsteady, queasy feeling even before she opens her mouth. This song, like the relationship it depicts, is clearly built on sand.

The track, though, had a skew-whiff and talented genius, unblinkingly painting a compelling and dysfunctional obsession with lurid honesty. Sly and shifting, Tricky's canny words hinted at a love that, tantalizingly, was to remain out of grasp: "This is sex without touching." Björk's fervent vocal, fittingly, sounds alternately enthusiastic and adrift.

A raw yet textured exercise in songwriting brilliance, it's probably futile to speculate to what degree 'Enjoy' represented Björk and Tricky chronicling their own intense yet short-lived affair. Björk, though, has frankly admitted its autobiographical genesis.

"My relationship with Tricky has a lot of energy, very raw," she divulged in the *Post* book. "'Enjoy' in a way was about, 'I wish: I want to stay here ...' but you have to move on. 'This is sex without touching...just enjoy.' That's very characteristic of our relationship."

had also attracted critical acclaim for some of his own visceral, intuitive rhythms, and was about to break big with the fascinating *Maxinquaye* album. In no time at all, Björk and Tricky had begun a relationship.

Tricky spent Christmas 1994 with Björk in Reykjavik, before she travelled to Nassau to begin recording *Post*, and in a matter of days the pair had composed two songs that found their way on to the album – 'Enjoy' and 'Headphones'.

"We drove around in a four-wheel drive and saw the glaciers and swam in the hot springs," Björk related to US magazine *Interview*. "It was brilliant working there – 24-hour darkness and snow."

It was clear that 'Enjoy' came as much from the insular, self-absorbed muse of Tricky as it did from Björk's musical vision. Tricky's awkward, shifty

06 You've Been Flirting Again

One of the slightest, most glancing pieces on *Post*, 'You've Been Flirting Again' was a solo Björk composition that she shaped into life together with Eumir Deodato.

Björk had originally become aware of Deodato through his classical strings arrangements for contemporary Latin music, and contacted him pre-*Post* to ask for his assistance. Deodato was much taken with the Björk *modus operandi*, telling Martin Aston in *Björkgraphy* that she had "developed a style and music that I've never heard anything like in my life."

Deodato originally met Björk in London before

the Nassau sessions to work together on two songs, 'Hyperballad' and 'Isobel'. These were completed so quickly that Björk decided to write a third piece, the engaging mini-suite that is 'You've Been Flirting Again', and played it to Deodato on the piano. The Brazilian then wrote out the score for an orchestra.

"That was my first string arrangement," Björk relates in the *Post* book. "That's what I'm probably most proud of on this album. I feel like I've just passed a maths test!"

'You've Been Flirting Again' is also significant in being Björk's first Nellee Hooper-less solo production credit, apart from 'The Anchor Song' which appeared on *Debut*. It's notable that both tracks are free of syncopated beats: clearly, Björk's developing mixing board skills didn't yet extend to her beloved electronica.

Instead, 'You've Been Flirting Again' is a muted, melancholic string piece wherein Björk, who spends most songs caught in the throes of extreme passion and giddy on life, for once plays the part of a calm, detached third party, advising a friend who has argued with his lover on how to reconcile and smooth the waters.

It may be hard to see Björk as a beatific agony aunt but her vocal is suitably soothing and encouraging and the debut string arrangement begins shy and distant before rising to a swelling, gentle climax. At 2 minutes and 29 seconds, 'You've Been Flirting Again' is one of the shortest tracks on *Post* but is certainly no trifling filler.

07 Isobel

A sweet yet rambling narrative akin to a surreal children's fairy tale, 'Isobel' had probably the most convoluted genesis of any song on Post, and arguably in the whole of Björk's *oeuvre*.

Björk co-wrote 'Isobel' with old friend Sigurjón B Sigurdsson, more commonly known as Sjón. They met while she was still in Kukl and Sjón was part of a Reykjavik anarcho-poetry syndicate named Medusa, together with Björk's ex-husband Thór. Becoming friends, the pair stayed in touch, and Sjón was to edit the lavish *Post* book that accompanied this album's release.

Björk had the initial idea for 'Isobel' after observing, one day late in 1994, a moth that landed on her shirt collar and stayed with her for most of a busy day. Feeling that it represented an omen of sort, she struggled to create a story and a character around the incident, but found words unusually hard to come by.

"I was going mad trying to write the lyric," she recalled in a TV documentary on her work. "The moth had put this character in my mind but I had basically written 900 pages in my diary and got nowhere near summing it up. So I called Sjón."

Over a bottle of red wine, Björk explained to Sjón her concept that the moth had been an emissary from "The Unexplained" bringing her a message. She had also named the creature Isobel, after string arranger Isobel Griffiths, with whom she was working on the album. Sjón then knitted the elements into a coherent storyline.

"It dawned on me … that Isobel was Nature, in a way," he explained in an article in *Post* named "Here Come The Warm Moths". "She just visited Björk and showed her presence." For Björk and Sjón, Isobel came to symbolize the impulsive, intuitive spirit that Björk in particular felt to be the true soul of art and, indeed, the correct response to life. They imagined Isobel as a fiery spirit raised in a wild forest who had once tried to live in the civilization of a larger city but failed to tame her passionate nature.

"Isobel is a woman who was born in a forest from a spark, not a mother or a father," Björk developed, spiralling into Roald Dahl territory. "When she grows up she finds that the pebbles on the forest floor are actually baby skyscrapers. So when she is a fully-grown woman she finds herself living in the city.

"Most people in the city are run by their heads and she is completely instinct-driven, which doesn't match very well. So she dances on tables naked and kisses the wrong people and falls in love with them and makes a lot of … emotional crashes. Isobel means well but ends up doing a lot of harm, so decides to go back to the forest."

Sjón and Björk then imagined Isobel, back in her woody lair, defiantly deciding that her feral attitude to life was actually the correct one and training a school of moths to spread her philosophy. Isobel then sends the creatures to visit people who are adopting too cerebral an approach toward life and reprimand them – hence the winged creature alighting on Björk's collar.

"Of course, a creature that came from The Unexplained wouldn't try to use logic on you!" Björk concluded, triumphantly. "It just goes 'Nana na nana' and confuses you!"

'Isobel' is a preposterous yet touching fable, then, and a poignant one; resigned never to meeting anybody who shares her exhilarating lust for life, Isobel is forced to stay in her lonely forest hideout, "married to herself". The tale, and the tune, clearly caught the imagination of the studio team, with Nellee Hooper and Marius De Vries both scoring writing co-credits for their contributions to the song.

Musically, the track is one of the most lustrous on *Post*, with Björk spinning the yarn in suitably breathless mode, Maurice Murphy providing a haunting opening trumpet motif, and Eumir Deodato once again supplying a rich, ravishing string arrangement. Released as the second UK single from the album in August 1995, 'Isobel' peaked at number 23.

08 Possibly Maybe

Even among the riches of *Post*, 'Possibly Maybe' is one of the smartest and most sensual tracks on the album. Alternately rapt and resigned, the song represented Björk's attempt to document fully the emotional whirlwind of her relationship with previous lover Stephane Sednaoui.

Björk and Sednaoui had first met when he filmed the monochrome New York video for 'Big Time Sensuality' in late 1993, then the full-length *Vessel* in 1994. Sednaoui was known as a volatile and flamboyant figure, and the couple's affair was by all accounts a tempestuous and turbulent one until they split shortly before the pre-production work on *Post*.

Showing her customary fascination and bemusement with the workings of love, Björk set out in the impressionistic 'Possibly Maybe' to itemize exactly how infatuation had descended upon Sednaoui and herself – and how it had then died.

"It was a nine-month period where I fell in love, went all the way to the bottom, found out it wasn't really love, went up again, walked out of the water, got a towel, dried myself and walked away," she explained in Sjón's *Post* book. "I was trying so hard to write about this period in my life, and it was so difficult."

Each verse of 'Possibly Maybe' represents a month in the Björk/Sednaoui affair, starting with sly seduction ("Your flirt finds me out") and proceeding to the idea of experimentation ("I wouldn't mind perhaps/Spending little time with you"). The mood is charged and superbly poised: will Björk take a chance with this known charmer? Possibly maybe …

Once the affair is in full swing, Björk delights in the febrile, feckless nature of her new partner, the "eruptions and disasters" resulting from his unpredictable nature. Initially, she loves the "electric shocks" but then, despairing, can no longer handle her beau's draining demands: "I'm exhausted, leave me alone." Yet the song, and the fling, ends

on a defiantly coquettish note as Björk fondly consigns her ex-lover to history, sucking her tongue in tribute.

Nellee Hooper and Marius De Vries provide a suitable ambient reverie for this dear account of love found and lost, which formed the fifth UK single off *Post* and peaked in the UK chart, in November 1996, at number 13.

09 I Miss You

If 'Possibly Maybe' was a pensive, nostalgic look back at a failed love affair, 'I Miss You' was its absolute polar opposite; a bubbling, excited preview of an all-consuming and passionate relationship to come.

This idea is somewhat of a Björk lyrical staple (the girl is nothing if not consistent), being previously explored on 'Big Time Sensuality' and (to a lesser degree) 'One Day' on *Debut*. 'I Miss You', though, is a full-on, heady anticipation of an imminent spectacular affair, a song written from the peak of heightened expectation.

Björk penned 'I Miss You' with DJ, producer, engineer and sometime collaborator Howie B, and explained eagerly how the song reflected her colleague's personality.

"That's very much Howie B's energy in the song," she said in the *Post* book. "Nervous, pant, pant, you haven't got time to do everything you want to do, over-enthusiasm. I told Howie I wanted an energetic, physical song, modern Latin music. I wanted him to do exactly what he wanted."

It's intriguing to note that Howie is another musician with whom Björk later enjoyed a romantic entanglement, and the pair are clearly on the same emotional wavelength on 'I Miss You'. There's a crackle of sexual chemistry in Howie's jittery, nervy electro-pulse, and Björk's eager, energetic vocal almost salivates with desire for her unknown suitor: "When will I get my cuddle? Who are you?"

'I Miss You' is a tremendous evocation of frustrated desire, lifted from twitchy irritation only by Talvin Singh's fluent tabla and some coarse, uplifting blares of brass. Craig McLean, then deputy editor of *The Face* magazine, brilliantly described the song as "like high-kicking crickets in a chorus line," and its comedic elements were realized in a video that dropped Björk into an animated adventure with her cartoon faves *Ren & Stimpy*.

Released in February 1997, 'I Miss You' was the sixth and last single from *Post*, and not even *Ren & Stimpy*'s efforts could lift it higher than number 36 in the UK.

ABOVE:
Howie B.

"I didn't feel as excited over doing another record," Hooper told Martin Aston in *Björkgraphy*. "I thought Björk knew enough to do it herself this time but she felt she needed some coverage."

Nevertheless, Hooper agreed to oversee the project and work as a "safety net" for Björk as she set about recruiting collaborators and assuming control of the recording process. This is the central image of 'Cover Me': Nellee Hooper acting as Björk's guardian and watching her back as she crawls into the unknown and, musically, strives to "prove the impossible really exists."

This typically dramatic image ("This is really dangerous," Björk breathes, at one point) was justified during the Bahamas sessions. Nellee Hooper sent Björk deep down into a cave with headphones and a long-lead microphone to record her vocal in a suitably risky environment. Surrounded by bats, the singer crawled on her hands and knees on the cave floor in the dark – not an enterprise that you would imagine, for example, Mariah Carey agreeing to undertake.

Sadly, this back-to-nature version was scrapped on Björk's return to London, when during her soul-searching about the Nassau sessions she decided that she wanted to re-record 'Cover Me' with a harpsichord and dulcimer supplying an eerie, if less authentic, backing. Nellee Hooper was not involved in this re-think.

10 Cover Me

The fractured, beguiling 'Cover Me' had its origins in a series of fairly anguished conversations between Björk and Nellee Hooper as the star began to plot her strategy for *Post*.

After the success of their "dream team" *Debut* venture, Björk had approached Nellee to repeat the process on *Post*, only to find that, despite his huge enthusiasm for the previous project, he was less keen to take the reins this time.

11 Headphones

Post's intimate, inner-space closer 'Headphones' was the second of the two tracks that Björk dreamed up with Tricky in Reykjavik over Christmas 1994, but had its origin in a far earlier transatlantic exchange of ideas.

'Headphones' is dedicated by Björk to Graham Massey in gratitude for the days in the very early 1990s when the pair would send each other tapes of musical ideas and innovative found noises to listen to via headphones.

"We're both like archeologists in music," said Massey. "On the tapes were very much things that have lasted because they don't stick to rules. Or just plain genius."

"Graham's tapes would save my life!" enthused a typically hyperbolic Björk. "I would wait until the evening, put my headphones on and listen to the songs, and it would be so nurturing to fall asleep to the music."

Björk had many moons ago written a slightly gauche but charming set of lyrics trying to pin down the cosy pleasure of falling asleep to Massey's tapes, and when Tricky played her a melody as a suggested basis for a song she suggested utilizing these existing words. The resulting drifting, weightless dream-pop was 'Headphones'.

Little more than a hint of keyboard and glancing "found" noises, 'Headphones' looks to reproduce the blissful, nebulous sensation of being semi-conscious at the very cusp of sleep. Perchance to dream? "I like this resonance," breathes Björk, "it elevates me. This is very interesting."

Five-and-a-half minutes of freeform, glorious electronic experimentation, the abstract 'Headphones' would have bemused any sing-a-long pop fan who purchased *Post* on the strength of 'It's Oh So Quiet' and was a hypnotic and fitting end to a fascinating album.

Post was released worldwide in June 1995, although not without an initial headache for Björk and her One Little Indian label. Her manager, Derek Birkett, had forgotten to clear a thirty-second sample at the start of 'Possibly Maybe' from an album by experimental electronic musician Scanner, aka Robin Rimbaud. Rimbaud was phlegmatic about the oversight, but still Birkett had to delete the album on release and then put it out again with the sample – of a mobile phone dialling tone – removed.

Such minor irritations couldn't halt the progress of what was a fine sophomore album, though. *Post* reached as high as number 2 in the UK album chart and, even more tellingly, made number 32 in the world's largest music market, the US. No longer a peripheral, alternative figure, it was clear that Björk's star was ever more in the ascendant.

1995

TELEGRAM

IN THE SUMMER OF 1995, AS BJÖRK PREPARED TO TAKE *POST* ON THE ROAD FOR HER SECOND SOLO WORLD TOUR, HER RECORD LABEL, ONE LITTLE INDIAN, WERE BUSY CO-ORDINATING AN INTRIGUING AND POTENTIALLY VERY LUCRATIVE SIDE-PROJECT: A REMIX ALBUM OF THE TRACKS ON *POST*.

Essentially a repetition of the low-profile, limited edition *Debut* project *All The Remixes From The Same Album For Those People Who Don't Buy White Labels*, the notion of a *Post* remix album found favour with Björk, who had always been a big fan of remix culture.

"I think it's really exciting if a friend takes your song another way," she has said, reflecting on the phenomenon. "Remixing is not this new thing. There's always been this tradition about doing many versions of the same song, just like there are many sides to one story. Besides, I've always had this soft spot for scientists…"

Thus every track from *Post*, with the exception of 'The Modern Things' and 'It's Oh So Quiet' (but with one addition, 'My Spine') was remixed by a

host of Björk collaborators for the slightly clunkily-named *Telegram* (a different kind of post: geddit?). Complete with a CD booklet of tremendous photos by Nobuyoshi Araki to satisfy the most ardent Björkophile, *Telegram* was released in November 1996 with a suitably *laissez-faire* foreword from Björk.

"I'd like to thank the remixers and tell them how honoured me and my songs are to have become ingredients on their mixing-desk," she wrote. "Ta."

She was more typically forthcoming, however, in a handful of interviews to promote the album. "Music is like sex," she declared. "Why have sex alone when you can do it with someone else?"

01 Possibly Maybe

Björk had long admired Leeds-based techno duo LFO (Low Frequency Oscillation), known to their moms as Mark Bell and Gez Varley. She had first approached them to be involved on *Debut*, only to find they were

RIGHT:
Leeds-based duo LFO.

LEFT:
The Brodsky
Quartet.

too busy. The respect was mutual, however, and LFO and Björk went on to pen 'I Go Humble', originally a B-side to 'Isobel' (*see* Chapter 10).

LFO totally dismantle the delicate 'Possibly Maybe' for their 'Lucy Mix', replacing the tentative reverie of the *Post* track with a grinding, inevitable techno beat and reducing Björk's winsome vocal to a distant ghost in the machine. Mark Bell, who was to prove a particularly compatible soul mate for Björk, went on to be the main producer on her 1997 *Homogenic* album.

02 Hyper-Ballad

For a reworking of *Post*'s enchanting 'Hyper-ballad', Björk turned to the Brodsky Quartet, an imaginative and experimental classical string quartet who had previously worked extensively with Elvis Costello. They eagerly replace the electronic bleeps and computer noises of the original with expansive violins, viola and cello.

"We wanted to slow down the tempo here, exhilarate there, just little things like that," explained violist Paul Cassidy in the *Post* book. "Björk's got a fantastic vocal technique. She was able to change her voice and put in nuances that we classical musicians think are reserved for us."

03 Enjoy

The Brodsky Quartet may have tip-toed relatively genteelly through 'Hyper-ballad', but techno renegades and Björk's labelmates Outcast drive a coach and horses through 'Enjoy' in one of *Telegram*'s most radical remixes, appropriately titled the 'Further Over The Edge' mix. Tricky had ensured the original's spiky, angular factor was high, but Outcast crush the song beneath a totalitarian, industrial beat, and by the end Björk is reduced to squealing "Jah!" like a particularly squeaky Rasta.

04 My Spine

'My Spine' is the cuckoo in the *Telegram* nest, being not just the only song that didn't feature on *Post* but also not even a remix, having featured in exactly the same format as a backing track to the 'It's Oh So Quiet' single. It can be assumed that Björk included it on *Telegram* either because she felt it was wasted as a b-side or, more prosaically, because something else fell through: a sub-standard mix of 'The Modern Things', perhaps?

'My Spine' shares writing and production credits between Björk and Evelyn Glennie, a Scottish avant-

than a conventional singing voice. That's special for me, as a musician. You feel you can do anything and the voice will be able to cope."

05 | I Miss You

'I Miss You' is transformed from the exuberant, joyous Björk/Howie B-penned skit on *Post* to a far moodier, trip-hop flavoured affair on *Telegram* by UK electronica maverick Dobie. Rodney P of hip-hop crew the London Posse adds a rapid-fire rap to the mix, transforming the mood of the song from eager anticipation to edgy disgruntlement.

Introduced to Björk by Tricky after producing Tricky's *Hell* EP collaboration with the Gravediggaz, Dobie later went on to record the acclaimed 1998 avant-jungle album *The Sound Of One Hand Clapping*, and 'I Miss You' is one of the most potent re-workings on the whole of *Telegram*.

06 | Isobel

Björk turned again to her much-loved Brazilian string arranger and conductor Eumir Deodato for a remix of the fanciful, fragile 'Isobel'. Deodato obliged with a richer, sparkier string-drenched version that also allowed a 20-piece orchestra to introduce fluid Latinate rhythms but still remained essentially faithful to the original's structure and dynamics.

07 You've Been Flirting Again

Björk clearly felt there was potential left unexplored in the *Post* version of this dreamy, drifting tune, and so reworked it herself for *Telegram*'s 'Flirt Is A Promise' mix.

This spacey remix exaggerates the original's

ABOVE:
***Percussionist,
Evelyn Glennie.***

garde classical percussionist who won a Grammy for her rendition of Bartok's *Sonata For Two Pianos And Percussion* despite have been clinically deaf from the age of twelve. This apparently crippling ailment has never prevented her from playing with most of the world's greatest orchestras.

This track is possibly for true Björk diehards only, featuring the star at her most cutesy and whimsical. Over the spindly, staccato sound of Glennie playing xylophone on car exhaust pipes, Björk recites a list of quirky features in boys that turn her on and send a pretty rush down her spine. Backs of necks score highly, as do "fascinating fingers". The reference to men "working creative" while, ahem, "touching their tools" is, it's probably safe to assume, an unfortunate consequence of Björk having to write lyrics in a second language.

Glennie, while acknowledging that 'My Spine' was concocted from no more than "car exhaust pipes laid on a frame", praised her co-performer fulsomely in the *Post* book: "Björk has a very instrumental voice, more like a musical instrument extremes. Björk introduces an eerie, echoing effect to the track's hesitant opening, emphasizing the sense of dilemma, before allowing Eumir Deodato to layer cinematic, sweeping strings beneath her vocal, as though the quarrelling lovers have achieved a joyous resolution.

08 Cover Me

An utterly transmuted 'Cover Me' is given a brutal junglist beating-up on *Telegram* by noted south London drum'n'bass innovator Dillinja.

Despite being an underground figure, Dillinja had recorded drum'n'bass tracks for more than ten labels by the mid-1990s, including Metalheadz, the seminal jungle label founded by Goldie. Unsurprisingly, he applies his hard-edged, uncompromising style to the minimalist 'Cover Me' to telling effect, an avalanche of belligerent beats replacing the haunting empty spaces of the original.

09 Army of Me

Post's thunderous opener 'Army Of Me' was, of course, co-written by Björk and Graham Massey, and the 808 State man's revision of the tune on *Telegram* is every bit as radical as Dillinja's pummelling mutilation of 'Cover Me'.

With Björk's vocal only a spasmodic, occasional element, Massey's mix recalls groundbreaking late European practitioners of industrial electronica of the 1980s such as SPK, Young Gods or Skinny Puppy, but it's questionable how many Björk fans would have appreciated the Mancunian throttling the life out of the tune.

10 Headphones

For 'Headphones', the closing track on *Telegram* – as it was on *Post* – Björk recruited arguably the most interesting collaborator on the entire album.

Mika Vainio is one-half of Finnish minimalist, hard house duo Panasonic, and also records solo material under the name Ø. Under this guise, his work tends toward what *allmusic.com* critic Sean Cooper calls "sparse machine noises, shifting rhythms, stubbornly unmusical sonic textures and assorted channel separation weirdness," and this is the sensibility that Vainio brought to 'Headphones'.

Consequently, his abstracted, nocturnal 'Ø mix' is even less at home to Mr Tune than was the Tricky/Björk original. If *Post*'s 'Headphones' carried the promise of sweet dreams, *Telegram*'s remix was likely to yield only nightmares.

Telegram was released in the UK in November 1996 with a minimum of fanfare or promotional support and reflected its non-commercial nature by failing to trouble the album chart compilers. When released in the States two months later, though, Björk fans who had warmed to *Post* far more than to *Debut* surprisingly lifted the record to number 66 in the *Billboard* chart. A transatlantic *Telegram* had been received.

1996

HOMOGENIC

As the *Telegram* side-project was falling into place in the second half of 1995, Björk was gearing herself up to take *Post* on tour — and was also, unknown to her, about to enter the most traumatic period of her career and life to date.

RIGHT:
Goldie: who developed an unlikely yet inevitable relationship with Björk.

Determined to avoid predictability, Björk decided that the *Post* tour would eschew taped and sampled material, relying instead on keyboardist Leila Arab manipulating overall sound via an onstage mixing-desk. The backdrop was equally risk-taking and unexpected, consisting of a futuristic forest of metallic sinister-yet-playful trees.

This brilliant, baroque presentation rolled across Europe playing sold-out arenas and festival dates during the autumn of 1995. On many of the dates, Björk was supported by arch junglist Goldie, the poster boy and icon of the UK drum'n'bass scene, and soon an unlikely yet somehow inevitable relationship developed between the pair.

Björk had by now ended her affair with Tricky, the commitment-phobic rapper, and when now-defunct UK monthly magazine *ikon* joined the Björk-and-Goldie tour on the road in Munich in September 1995, it found them getting on just fine.

"People ask me why I'm on the road with Goldie and I don't understand the question," Björk reflected. "Am I supposed to be with the fucking Cranberries, or playing stadiums with REM? They don't interest me. Goldie has loads of energy, and he's full-on and very happy, and that's what I'm always looking for."

Goldie, for his part, rhapsodized his touring partner's vocal ability. "I listen to Björk perform every night, all the energies she puts into her voice, and it's like a glass," he wondered. "It makes me feel so vulnerable. I think, 'Shit, she's going to break the glass!' She pushes it so hard, every night ..."

Indeed. A few weeks later, as *Post* hit the States, Björk *did* break the glass, being forced to cancel four shows in California with vocal problems. By now, though, she and Goldie were very firmly an item. "I feel like I'm on natural E," she told UK style magazine *Dazed & Confused*, discussing her new relationship.

Rumours abounded on the Internet that Björk and Goldie were contemplating marriage as the *Post* tour, now minus her beau, swung into southeast Asia. Yet all was not rosy in Björk's garden.

Too many months on the road plus life in the public eye were bugging her, and she was soon to snap spectacularly.

When Björk arrived in Bangkok airport in February 1996, she was greeted by an unwanted journalist, Julie Kaufman, who bid her "Welcome to Bangkok" and tried to interview her. It was, at most, a minor irritation, but a stressed-out Björk reacted by hurling Kaufman to the ground and smashing her head against the floor.

Björk apologized to Kaufman the next day and One Little Indian issued an official statement, describing their star as "physically and mentally exhausted" and saying the incident was "out of character". Björk completed the tour and then vanished with Goldie for a recuperative vacation in the Maldives.

The singer had a relatively relaxed summer of 1996, except for picking up a slew of awards and appearing at festivals such as San Francisco's Free Tibet event. However, as autumn dawned a terrible development was to shatter her precious, short-lived equilibrium.

Ricardo Lopez was a 21-year-old Miami-based loner and Björk fanatic who objected strongly on racist grounds to the singer's relationship with Goldie. In September 1996, he videotaped himself talking about Björk while posting to her London address a book booby-trapped to spray sulphuric acid when opened. Then, with 'I Miss You' playing in the background and the video camera still running, he blew his head off with a shotgun.

The grisly package never reached its target. Florida police, alerted by the smell from Lopez's apartment, discovered his decom-

posing body, viewed the videotape, and alerted their London counterparts who intercepted the package. Unsurprisingly, though, Björk was profoundly upset by the episode.

"People have to realize not to get so obsessed about me," she told paparazzi waiting outside her home when the media broke the story. "I'm just a singer who sings pop songs. That's all."

Life in the goldfish bowl of fame had never terribly suited the fiercely independent Björk, and the gruesome Lopez incident was the last straw. She had always felt ambivalent, at best, toward life in London, and regarded even a relatively small degree of press intrusion into her privacy as intolerable. The need to begin recording the follow-up to *Post* offered her the possibility of escape.

LEFT:
Ricardo Lopez: his obsession with Björk reached a terrible conclusion.

As 1997 dawned, Björk decamped to the mountain-top El Cortijo studio on the southern coast of Spain with Mark Bell from LFO, her new-found musical partner-in-crime who was to oversee and co-produce the majority of her new venture. Bell was an appropriate choice, for after the lush musical variety of *Debut* and *Post*, Björk was keen to strip her muse back to basics – a move she equated, basically, with a return to her roots.

"I decided really early that this album was just going to be beats, strings and my voice," she declared. "And the beats should be very simple, almost naïve, but still very natural and explosive, like they're still in the making – which, to me, is very much the nature of Iceland."

This musical minimalism also, at an early stage, spawned the album's title. "I'm calling it *Homogenic* because it's just one flavour: me, here, now," Björk reflected. "*Debut* and *Post* were like me playing in a toy store, going haywire and indulging all of my musical passions. I was getting rid of my back catalogue.

"Those two albums were like the Tin Tin books – *Tin Tin Goes To Congo*, or *Tin Tin Goes To Tibet*," she extemporized, slightly bafflingly. "*Homogenic* is more like Björk going home, going back to Iceland and what I'm all about."

Bell and Björk set to work, and soon hit on a productive working method. Bell was a big fan of writing tunes and melodies on mini-DAT machines, and soon schooled his eager pupil in their merits. Björk was delighted at the flexibility they granted her, enthusing that they gave her scope to create "on an aeroplane, at your gran's house, or on top of a volcano."

Embracing such spontaneity and musical minimal-ism, Björk was also able to continue the habit of *al fresco* creativity she had developed with Nellee Hooper in the Bahamas during the recording of *Post*. This time, she wasn't just singing on the beach; her DAT enabled her actually to write the songs there.

In a scenario hugely reminiscent of 'Hyper-ballad', Björk began most working days by walking along the cliffs by her Spanish hideout, taking in nature and collecting her thoughts before she decamped to the studio for the day.

"I could see Africa!" she enthused later, looking back at her privileged setting. "There's something very special about living on the edge of continents. When I lived by the ocean in Iceland, I used to walk every morning for an hour and it helped me work. It was the same recording *Homogenic*."

Given the traumatic events leading up to its recording, and Björk's declared wish to make a record that evoked the primal, brooding nature of Iceland's landscapes, it was scarcely a surprise that *Homogenic* proved to be her darkest and rawest album to date. Any observers who still regarded Björk as a whimsical, chirpy pop pixie were about to be very surprised indeed.

01 Hunter

Nowhere was Björk's desire to celebrate the feral, elemental splendour of Iceland clearer than on *Homogenic*'s opening track, the stark, icy 'Hunter'.

Co-produced, like the majority of the album, by Björk and Mark Bell, 'Hunter' is a tremulous, agitated surge of electronica wrapped around the beauteous symphonic strings of the Icelandic String Octet. Björk had chosen to use only Icelandic players, hoping their innate, intuitive understanding of the nation would help achieve the native, naturalistic mood she craved. At least one of them picked up on her quest.

"Some Icelandic composers, when they compose Icelandic music, try to imitate geysers and volcanoes," said Sigurbjorn Bernhardsson, a violinist in the Icelandic String Octet. "Björk wanted the rough sound of wind, storms, the landscape, not a smooth European sound.

"I picked up her use of fifths straight away," he continued. "Fifths are very traditional in Icelandic folk music. On 'Hunter' the two cellos are playing a two-bar motif; one plays the lower notes, one plays a fifth above. As soon as you hear that, you know right away this is Icelandic music."

'Hunter' opens around a speedy, semi-militaristic beat over which Björk states a defiant, individualistic manifesto: "If travel is searching/ And home what's been found/I'm not stopping …" The image of herself as a hunter, fearlessly foraging for sustenance and new experiences, is both in line with *Homogenic*'s survivalist ethos and previous lyrical adventures such as *Post*'s 'Cover Me'.

It soon becomes clear, though, that like much of *Homogenic*, 'Hunter' is concerned with a failed relationship. Björk"s affair with Goldie, which she had described as her "strongest for years" had come to an end just prior to the album's recording sessions and there is little doubt she is smarting. Left "… on my own/To complete the mission", Björk appears determined to tough it out through the pain.

The scornful lyrical reference to her foolishness in trying to regulate and organize freedom ("How

Scandinavian of me!") is an interesting one. In Björk's personal lexicon, "Scandinavian" invariably refers to an over-analytical, logical worldview in which passions and instincts are sidelined; the exact opposite to her own heady, impulsive personal philosophy.

Tellingly, the sleeve booklet to *Homogenic* lists a final lyric, repeated twice: "You just didn't know me!" Doubtless aimed at Goldie, these words can't be heard on the track, which is finally buffed into a glorious shine by Björk's trusty string arranger Eumir Deodato.

When released as the second single from *Homogenic*, in December 1998, 'Hunter' fell just short of the UK Top 40 at number 44.

02 Jóga

Björk has never been afraid to be awkwardly over-literal in declaring her musical and philosophical agendas, and 'Jóga' is the most direct statement on *Homogenic* of the musical mission she undertook on the album.

Dedicated to her closest friend in Iceland, the Jóga to whom *Post* was joint-dedicated, this string-guided track is a mass of electronic explosions and eruptions which set out to reproduce the spectacular seismic shifts and spurting geysers of Iceland. Björk correlates these natural wonders with her own turbulent, troubled "emotional landscapes", which only Jóga is able to understand fully and empathize with.

Describing 'Jóga' as a "stark, simple, friend-to-friend thing", Björk also confirmed her attempt to evoke Iceland's volcanic vistas in music. "Iceland is geographically the youngest country on the planet," she said. "It's still developing, and growing, and changing and very raw. There's a lot of energy there, and I wanted the beats on 'Jóga' to be like that."

The Icelandic String Octet again provide a succulent, swooping counterpoint to Mark Bell's earthy, exploding samples and programming, on which

LEFT:
Björk and Goldie's relationship ended just prior to the Homogenic *sessions.*

established Björk collaborator Howie B also lends a hand. The Iceland factor is enhanced further still by Sjón, Björk's long-time Reykjavik friend and co-author of "Isobel", scoring a writing credit.

The back-to-Icelandic-nature theme of 'Joga' was made even starker by a video, taken from a helicopter, that showed Björk alone on one of the nation's spectacular snowscapes as the camera swooped over the impossible, eye-boggling vistas and portrayed the natural extremity, or "state of emergency". The track was released as a limited-edition single, a gambit which Björk made a typically idiosyncratic and inventive bid to rational-ize in aesthetic terms.

"There's something about 'Joga' which is very precious to me," she told British TV show *The O-Zone*. "It's a very intimate, personal song, so I guess the decision to make the single a limited edition was Derek [Birkett, One Little Indian boss] listening to me tell him how I feel about the song, then translating that into business terms."

03 Unravel

Co-written and co-produced by Björk and her frequent musical associate Guy Sigsworth, 'Unravel' is a morose, saddened musing on the pain occasioned by being separated from a lover, whether by geography or emotional distance.

Sigsworth hits a mournful, regretful organ riff and stays there as Björk, alone and adrift, addresses her absent partner; "While you are away/My heart comes undone." The song unfolds at a funereal pace, the elegiac reverie interrupted only by spasmodic, occasional flurries of keyboard which disturb the eloquent heartache.

This is prime Björk lyrical territory, of course, as previously explored on 'Aeroplane' or 'I Miss You', but while those songs looked forward excitedly to the ending of the temporary state of exile, 'Unravel' is infinitely more pessimistic. As Björk's heart unravels in her lover's absence, the devil rolls it into "a ball of yarn" which he refuses to return: this love appears doomed.

Sigsworth's melancholic organ sounds the very image of hopelessness as 'Unravel' describes a spiral of emotional despair; the climactic wish that Björk and her beau will "make new love" sounds a remote possibility. Björk has never gone on record to confirm that 'Unravel' was aimed at recently-departed lover Goldie, but this appears highly probable.

04
Bachelorette

Lavish, cinematic and, to adopt one of Björk's own favourite compliments, *gorgeous*, 'Bachelorette' was seized on by most critics as the stand-out track on *Homogenic*, and one of the most beautiful pieces of music Björk has ever produced.

'Bachelorette' was co-written by Björk and her fellow Icelandic conspirator Sjón, and works as a narrative and musical sequel to *Post*'s fanciful 'Isobel', which was also collaboration between the pair. Sjón provided the dramatic, image-rich poetry for the storyline of the song, but the measured, magnificently evocative music was all Björk.

'Isobel' had ended with the song's eponymous heroine, unable to live in the cold and cerebral city because of her hot-blooded, spontaneous nature, retreating back to her native forest to avoid damaging more lives. Despite this withdrawal, Björk has explained, Isobel never doubted that her passion-

ate, intuitive approach to life was the most rewarding one. She always knew she was right.

"So on 'Bachelorette', Isobel decides to return to the city," Björk concluded. "It's like the sequel to her story. She goes back to the city on the train, which is why the beats of the song are like a train, and she prepares to confront all the people that she loves with … love. It's a disarming confrontation."

Björk also described 'Bachelorette' as "a cut-the-crap sort of thing" but in truth the mood of the song is far from stark minimalism. 'Bachelorette' is staggering in both its lyrical and musical detail and imagination, from the train-track electro-rhythms at the song's outset to Eumir Deodato's sublime instrumentation to an utterly radiant vocal display from Björk. She had truly never been in better voice.

'Bachelorette' is alive with arresting images, from the Isobel/Björk figure as "a fountain of blood/In the shape of a girl" to the lost, forlorn ex-lover circling, adrift and aimless, "like a killer whale/Trapped in a bay". It's a work of fantastical invention, and Björk proved laudably determined to share the credit for it.

"I talked to Sjón about the song, and he just came straight out with all these brilliant ideas like a tree that grows hearts," she marvelled. "'Bachelorette' is definitely me and my mate getting all over-romantic."

The expressive romanticism of Sjón's imagery was mirrored and furthered by Björk's febrile production: 'Bachelorette' is the only song on *Homogenic* for which she takes sole producer credit. Released, deservedly, as the lead-off

single from the album in December 1997, 'Bachelorette' reached number 21 in the UK chart.

05 All Neon Like

Abstracted and womb-like, 'All Neon Like' is an obsessive, hypnotic doodle that finds Björk hymning a distracted beauty from somewhere deep in a netherworld.

The song unwinds around one deep, muffled yet insidious electro-pulse, as if Björk is delivering this singular bulletin from the other side from deep within some alien yet benign being. There are strong echoes of 'Headphones' from *Post* in the way that she abandons the constrictions of the song to, instead, explore a maze of textures; the lyrical imagery also looks forward to 'Cocoon' from *Vespertine*.

If it forms part of Björk's central *Homogenic* motif of celebrating Iceland's volatile, voluptuous nature, then 'All Neon Like' is positively subterranean, a lullaby delivered from a fairy grotto deep beneath the permafrost of the tundra and fjords. This is the first track on *Homogenic* on which LFO man Mark Bell's distinctive production hand is easily detectable among the repetitive, seductive ambient beats.

06 5 Years

There could hardly be a more pronounced contrast on *Homogenic* between the soft, nurturing 'All Neon Like' and the following track, the cold-eyed, vengeful slice of techno-rage that is '5 Years'.

Almost certainly aimed at the retreating back of recently departed paramour Goldie, '5 Years' opens in a scornful, simmering strop as Björk berates her ex-lover over a suitably belligerent hardcore techno backing. "You're the one that's missing out" she informs her deserter, predicting that this truth will only hit home to him in five years time when he wakes up "all love-less".

hapless soul who, unforgivably, has proven unworthy of her adoration.

"There is a purpose in the drums being really hard and the voice beautiful, and that's the contrast value," said Bell, discussing '5 Years'. "For something to be beautiful, something else has to be ugly. If everything is beautiful, then nothing is beautiful."

If nothing else, the ferocious, fiery ire ladled on the inadequate suitor during the course of '5 Years' tended to suggest that Björk, in relationships, was definitely no picnic.

"I'm probably a full-time job for somebody," Björk conceded on the release of *Homogenic*, when quizzed on this point. "I'm no holiday. I tend to be always on – I'm either totally happy or totally upset or totally stupid. And I'm always brutally honest, which can be a good thing or a terrible thing."

It's rare to hear ire and irritation as the chief emotions of a Björk ditty, but as a sharp-edged condemnation of a failed lover, '5 Years' is unsurpassable, which makes it highly surprising that Goldie received a sleeve note "Thank you" on *Homogenic*. For all her sudden temper, Björk is clearly a forgiving soul at heart.

07 Immature

If '5 Years' was Björk's knee-jerk, cathartic outburst of rage at the fast-exiting Goldie, 'Immature' was the slow, reflective comedown that follows the end of any intensive relationship as the participants rake over its demise and, inevitably, seek to apportion blame.

The slight, wounded 'Immature' finds Björk castigating herself for her gullibility and naïvety in investing trust in a lover who ultimately, she feels, proved unworthy. It's a deep sigh of anguished self-accusation: "How could I be so immature/To think he would replace/The missing elements in me?" For all of her much-vaunted fierce independence, Björk clearly feels deeply the ache of abandonment.

ABOVE:
Goldie: target of Björk's rage in '5 Years'.

Björk has always forcefully expressed the belief that committing to a love affair is a rewarding act of bravery ("It takes courage/To enjoy it", as 'Big Time Sensuality' has it) but her latest partner has committed the cardinal sin of timidity, arousing her angry contempt ("I'm so bored of cowards"). Mark Bell's seething techno-backing spits and hums like molten lava as Björk reproaches the

Musically, 'Immature' is a clatter of syncopated beats rattling around some lovely scattered found noises and unusual instrumentation. Björk utilizes unorthodox implements throughout *Homogenic*, and Alasdair Malloy's glass harmonica is particularly bewitching here.

08
Alarm Call

After the emotional desolation of '5 Years' and 'Immature', the perky dance-pop of 'Alarm Call' seems somewhat incongruous on *Homogenic*, almost as if the tune were a left-over from the more upbeat *Post* sessions.

'Alarm Call' could easily, in fact, be a techno-sussed sibling of 'Human Behaviour' in its wide-eyed, eager affirmation of the positive qualities of the quixotic yet fascinating human species that Björk has always chronicled so avidly. "I have walked this earth and watched people", she asserts, like a visiting alien dignitary. "I can be sincere and say I like them."

The song also revisits another perennial Björkian preoccupation, of getting back to nature to listen to extreme, fantastic music (remember the "little ghetto-blaster" of 'There's More To Life Than This'?). There are also echoes of the cliff-walking survivalist of 'Hyper-ballad', although on 'Alarm Call' Björk introduces humour into the equation, suggesting her happy ditties may bring about world peace.

The comedy – a relatively rare quality in Björk's music as she much prefers profound joy – continues as she declares that she's no "fucking

Buddhist" but she has found enlightenment, after which she recites a series of mildly Zen-like aphorisms exhorting the listener to awake to the joys of the moment.

The mood of 'Alarm Call' may be relatively uplifting by *Homogenic*'s standards but musically the track is entirely typical, with Björk's candid musings and vocal quirks given a grinding, sensual techno seeing-to by LFO man Bell. Released as a single in December 1998, it charted in the UK at number 33.

09 Pluto

Björk albums invariably become far less conventionally song-bound and much more wilfully abstracted as they near their culmination, and the jagged, ferocious 'Pluto' continued this tendency on *Homogenic*.

'Pluto' is the sole joint-composition on *Homogenic* between Björk and Mark Bell, and functions around a relatively formulaic industrial techno backbeat. There, however, the orthodoxy ends, as the co-conspirators cook up a sonic freak-out of bubbling, effervescent rhythms, keyboard alarums and excursions, brutalist drums and mangled snatches of the Icelandic String Octet.

Bell, cleverly, uses Björk's superhuman squeals and exhortations as just one more instrument in the mix, another colour on his palette. Björk, for her part, is in over-stimulated, hyperventilating mode, venting equal parts elation and vexation at the world around her. "Excuse me," she rasps, "but I just have to explode."

By the end of her vocal entreaties, Björk"s altered, treated and twisted-to-extremes vocal sounds scarcely human. She's always been good at communicating sheer, giddy, insatiable elation (cf: 'Violently Happy' / 'Big Time Sensuality') but this dark, brooding euphoria was something else again.

10
All is Full of Love

After the disturbed, troubled nature of much of *Homogenic*, and particularly the irate desolation of the post-Goldie songs, 'All Is Full Of Love'appeared to reassure anxious observers that all remained well in Björkworld.

A shimmering, textured electro-eulogy to the benevolence of existence, 'All Is Full Of Love' finds Björk offering care and guidance to a misguided, solitary soul temporarily weighed down by the world. Similar in tone to 'Come To Me' from *Debut*, the song has Björk offering nurturing, compassionate hope like a musical Samaritans: "You'll be given love/You'll be taken care of."

It's conceivable that the song could be one last regretful parting note delivered to the door of Goldie. "Your phone is off the hook" Björk rues, "Your doors are all shut." Yet the message of 'All Is Full Of Love' – in stark contrast to the malice of '5 Years' – is enlightened and forgiving. Björk, hurt but healing, is looking forward to a new day.

'All Is Full Of Love' was produced and mixed by Howie B, with whom it's widely believed Björk had a short romance around the recording of *Homogenic* – a belief that was encouraged when, together with her best friend Jóga and son Sindri, he was given a dedication on the album.

A most unlikely final single from *Homogenic*, 'All Is Full Of Love' was released in June 1999, almost two years after its parent album, and reached number 24 in the UK.

Wrapped in a striking computer-enhanced Nick Knight photograph of Björk, styled by Alexander McQueen, looking part-Oriental geisha queen, part extra-terrestrial fashion victim, *Homogenic* was released worldwide in September 1997. Greeted with Björk's customary adulatory reviews, it charted at number 4 in the UK and a highest-to-date number 28 in the States.

In the interviews surrounding the album's

release, Björk looked back at her *annus horribilis* of paparazzi intrusion, murder attempts by demented fans and failed love affairs and decided, defiantly, that that which did not kill her had made her stronger.

"My theory is that when I left Iceland, I had an unconscious wish that I wanted danger," she reflected. "Well, I asked for it and I got it – but a lot of the things that happened to me were self-inflicted. A car didn't drive over me. My child didn't get killed. People think I'm feeling sorry for myself – but I'm not."

Nevertheless, London had seen the last of Björk for a little while. Shortly after the release of *Homogenic*, as 1997 drew to a close, the singer returned to her native Reykjavik. The English adventure had run its course.

1998

SELMASONGS

**'I've Seen it All'
Selma (Björk) on
the flatbed truck.**

AFTER SPENDING THE MAJORITY OF 1998 TOURING *HOMOGENIC* AROUND THE GLOBE, BJÖRK RETURNED TO HER NATIVE REYKJAVIK TO PLAN HER NEXT MOVE. SHE WOULD HAVE FOUND IT IMPOSSIBLE TO PREDICT EXACTLY WHAT THIS WAS TO BE.

Toward the end of the year, Björk was contacted by Danish film-maker Lars Von Trier. Von Trier had noticed Björk in Spike Jonze's vivacious mock-1940s musical video for 'It's Oh So Quiet' and decided instantly that the singer was precisely what he required for his next major project.

"I was completely fascinated by her," he said. "The video just screamed right out that this person had to be a film star."

Björk had never heard of Von Trier, despite his reputation as an *enfant terrible* of the European arthouse movie circuit. Nonetheless, the Dane boasted an impressive resumé. His celebrated *Breaking The Waves* had won the Grand Prix du Jury at Cannes in 1996, and his follow-up movie, 1998's *The Idiots*, had been filmed within the purist "vow of chastity" of the Dogma theoretical school of directors.

Björk had never been attracted by acting, and politely declined Von Trier's invitation. Her resolve wavered, however, when he persevered and sent her the script for *Dancer In The Dark*, a powerful, bleak musical based on the tribulations of a Czech immigrant to the US called Selma.

"The offer came at the exact right time," she reflected later. "I had been writing about my own feelings by then for three albums, which is quite narcissistic, and it felt good to have the chance to write about Selma instead."

RIGHT:
Lars von Trier.

Selma (Björk) and Kathy (Catherine Deneuve) in Dancer in the Dark.

Björk agreed to compose the original sound-track to the movie, while continuing to rebuff Von Trier's entreaties to take the role of Selma. It was clear, though, that the character of Selma had struck a chord deep within her. "My immediate reaction to the script was very emotional," she said. "I agreed to write the songs from a very emotional point of view, as more a form of love for Selma than anything else."

It would have been a hard heart indeed that didn't melt at the plight of Selma Jezkova, the doomed heroine of *Dancer In The Dark*. A 30-year-old immigrant single mother living in Washington state, she has a terrible secret: she is going blind due to a hereditary eye disease, and her 10-year-old son, Gene, will inevitably suffer the same terrible fate.

Selma works a machine at a local factory making stainless steel sinks and, in her spare time, supplements her income with menial piece-work. Every single dollar she earns is stashed away in a hiding place in the trailer home that she and Gene rent from a local policeman, Bill, and his wife Linda.

Bill confides in Selma that his spendthrift wife has over-stretched their finances and the couple face having their property repossessed. Selma, in return, tells Bill about her imminent blindness, and the small fortune she is stashing away to pay for Gene's eye operation. The pair part with a vow to keep quiet about these confidences.

Selma's eyesight is continuing to deteriorate, and after she makes a bad mistake on the industrial machinery at work, she is sacked from her job. Arriving home with her final pay cheque, she discovers that Bill has sneaked into her home and stolen the cash that she had stashed away for her son.

Selma confronts a guilt-laden Bill about the theft and, in a terrible accident, shoots him with his police gun. Bill begs her to kill him, and she obliges. Arrested for the murder, Selma finds the jury unimpressed with her case for the defence, and she is sentenced to death. The film ends with some truly harrowing scenes.

RIGHT:
*Björk and von
Trier: frequently
at loggerheads.*

It is unlikely that this grisly tale would have held any great attraction for Björk were it not for the movie's musical content. In a charming and idiosyncratic sub-plot, the naïve and ingenuous Selma is a huge fan of melodramatic stage musicals, and breaks into a spectacular song-and-dance routine at the slightest opportunity.

Selma daydreams that the whirring, clanking kilns and furnaces at work are playing a Rodgers & Hammerstein-style tune to her: she hears musical rhythm in the motion of a train. She is even, with her best friend Kathy (Catherine Deneuve), taking part in an amateur dramatic production of *The Sound Of Music*, although her failing eyesight forces her to abandon that side-project.

Björk, intrigued by this coquettish and fanciful character, admitted that there were similarities between her own character and the fragile, other-worldly Selma. "We both feel more comfortable inside a song than we do in real life," she mused.

"There's a great deal of escape from reality in both Selma and me. I only feel safe and calm when I make music and sing. The only difference is that Selma is more naïve than me because she really thinks life can be one long musical, and I don't think that any longer."

Her curiosity in this perverse new project aroused, Björk set to composing the music for Selma's fantasy sequences in *Dancer In The Dark*. Her first efforts were returned to her by Von Trier, as the notoriously difficult-to-please director wasn't satisfied with her efforts. He also renewed his efforts to persuade Björk to play Selma.

"I told Lars I had never played theatre before, and I hadn't got the tiniest scrap of acting ambition in me," Björk said. "I'm not in the slightest excited about being an actress. But I started to feel so much for this poor girl, Selma, and I decided that maybe I should fight for her, and her songs, with my life.

"Maybe this role was in a way designed for me,"

she concluded, finally. "I think Lars saw something in me that was perfect for it. I haven't dared to ask him what."

So Björk was now officially Selma, and reworked the movie's soundtrack to fit Von Trier's demanding specifications. On May 17, 1999, the shooting of *Dancer In The Dark* began in the Swedish town of Trollhättan, the fulcrum of the Scandinavian movie world that was known locally as Trollywood.

By conventional standards, *Dancer In The Dark* was shot extraordinarily quickly, with the whole movie filmed in little more than three months. This did not mean, however, that the production was a pain-free process. It soon became apparent that Björk, who was famously incapable of giving less than her all to the creative process, was becoming rather more involved with Selma than was possibly desirable.

"It has meant a lot of conflicts for Björk," said Catherine Deneuve, acknowledging the unique perspective her co-star had brought to the movie. "Her empathy for the role is total. She is not a trained actress, and maybe doesn't have the same ability as us to go in and out of the roles we play. She identified herself so much with Selma that it has become hard for her to bear."

There was also a succession of stories leaking from the set indicating that Björk and the wilful, headstrong Von Trier were finding their working relationship difficult. Björk, who talked of "defending" her character, seems to have taken the Stanislavsky school of method acting to the nth degree. One journalist who visited the set found Von Trier communicating with his star only via the choreographer: "If I tell her to do something, she just does the opposite," the director complained.

However, the huge row that blew up between Björk and Von Trier, and which led to the singer vacating the set, wasn't down to acting theory but, inevitably, music. Björk had not signed a contract with the director regarding control over the film's score and, to her horror, found that he was altering and editing her music – as was his right.

Björk flew into a rage and walked off the set. It's likely that the story that made the newspapers that she attempted to eat her dress in her anger is apocryphal, but she still refused to resume filming until Von Trier had reluctantly signed a "manifesto" that she wrote ensuring that she wielded complete creative control over the soundtrack.

Harmony thus restored, shooting transferred to Copenhagen, ending in July. By then, Von Trier's demanding and exhaustive filming techniques – he insisted, for example, that all of Björk's song-and-dance routines were filmed by one hundred cameras – had made *Dancer In The Dark* the most expensive Scandinavian movie in history.

Bleak, relentless and unforgiving, *Dancer In The Dark* was one of the most extreme pieces of cinema to secure a mainstream release in years, and Björk's powerful and passionate score provided one of its most distinctive features.

Unsurprisingly, she drafted in a few old allies to finesse the soundtrack. Mark Bell again oversaw programing, while Guy Sigsworth and Isobel Griffiths were once more involved in arrangements. From Iceland, Valgeir Sigurdsson engineered the music in Reykjavik and the trusty Sjón again weighed in with lyrics.

01 Overture

Both musically and visually, the overture to *Dancer In The Dark* opens with a stark, blanched minimalism before building to a vivid, vibrant slash of rich scarlets and oranges. Conducted, as is the entire score, by Vincent Mendoza, it's a short orchestral piece that begins hesitantly, with a nervous, wary parp of brass before some rousing timpani lends this scene-setting solo Björk composition a resonant minor majesty as the cinema audience takes its seat and shuffles its popcorn.

02 Cvalda

Selma's musical interludes in *Dancer In The Dark* function as fantasy sequences and escapism from her increasingly desperate fate, so the first number, 'Cvalda', doesn't appear until over half an hour into the movie – which doesn't prevent it being one of the most striking and memorable images of the entire film.

Desperate to earn extra funds to finance Gene's treatment, Selma has taken a night shift in the factory, to the horror of her friend Kathy, who realizes that Selma's eyesight is far worse than she

is letting on. Kathy arrives, unpaid, to help the dreamy and over-tired Czech girl perform her duties.

Every *Dancer In The Dark* song begins with Selma's febrile, over-heated musical imagination turning every-day sounds into music. In 'Cvalda', as the presses crash and the steel sinks clatter, she mentally trans-forms the factory floor into a stage musical and her production line colleagues become a high-kicking, gyrating chorus line to the machine symphony.' Cvalda' is Selma's affectionate nickname for Kathy: "It means someone who is big and happy," she tells her friend. As the track begins, Selma emphasizes and accentuates the rhythm of the factory machines with the wordless, formless song language at which Björk is so adept: "Clatter, crash, clack, cricket bang sun" is the most accurate transcription. Then she addresses her colleague, continuing a dialogue in-joke between the pair: "Cvalda/You're the dancer ..."

Mark Bell's hard-edged, uncompromising programing soon gives way to a far more expansive tone as 'Cvalda' blossoms into a fully-blown song

from the shows, Björk letting rip with her full vocal range as she serenades her best friend and hymns the machines that are lifting her out of her constrictions: "What a beautiful sound."

'Cvalda' is a duet with Catherine Deneuve, and in the movie the pair form the centre of a dance that mimics the repetitive motions of the industrial machinery around them. As the tune builds to a Broadway climax the dancing becomes ever-more spectacular, a riot of backflips and somersaults mirroring the theatrical extravagance. The mood is pure *West Side Story*, Von Trier's favourite musical. Only as the song fades do we see that Selma, distracted and daydreaming, has neglected her machine and broken it – the mistake that leads to her dismissal.

'Cvalda' offers glaring clues to the reasons why Von Trier was so desperate for Björk to take the lead in his movie, and her natural empathy for the part. Throughout her career, Björk has steadfastly maintained that the most entrancing, transforming music is the cacophony of sound that is heard around us every day. *Dancer In The Dark* gave her a rare chance to make the philosophy concrete.

"One thousand years ago in Africa, music was about taking the magic of the noises you hear every day and taking it to the next level, which is making a tune out of it," she has said. "The Africans would make songs out of bird noises and rhythms and rivers. Their music sounded like their lives.

"It was the same in America in the 1950s. Everybody was driving round in these big cars that went 'VROOM VROOM VROOM!' so of course they invented rock'n'roll, which made the same noise! That's what music is – realism, magic realism, taking what is surrounding us each day and making it magic."

'Cvalda' is a musical co-composition between Björk and Mark Bell, with the singer getting together with Sjón and also Von Trier to write the lyrics. "I don't think Björk was too thrilled by my attempts as a lyricist," the director later reflected. "But she was still loyal enough to perform them anyway."

03 I've Seen It All

The poignant, almost unbearably bittersweet 'I've Seen It All' is another duet, and one of the most beautiful and immaculately constructed tracks on *Dancer In The Dark*. In the movie, Selma sings the number with her hulking suitor Jeff, played by Peter Stormare, but for the album she found another partner in Radiohead frontman Thom Yorke.

The film context is that Selma, her eyesight deteriorating virtually daily, has been fired from the foundry. Too short-sighted to cycle, she has no option but to attempt to walk home along a railway line, feeling her way with the outside of her foot against the track. As Jeff runs after her a trains traps her on the bridge, nearly crushing her to death. A concerned Jeff, noting her near-blindness, asks bluntly, "You can't see, can you?" to which a hurt, defensive Selma whispers, "What is there to see?".

In typical escapist mode, Selma escapes the stresses of the situation by imagining another big musical number, this time triggered by the rhythms of the passing train. In tilted, singsong tones, she recites a litany of wondrous, everyday sights that she has enjoyed in her life, Björk's "magic realism" in full effect: "I've seen it all, I have seen the trees/I have seen the willow leaves dancing in the breeze."

In *Dancer In The Dark*, Selma and Jeff climb on the flatbed train, and Stormare proves a game but somewhat inadequate vocal partner as he chides Selma that the world contains so much she has yet to see ("elephants, kings or Peru") only to hear her reply that she has "better to do". The mood is playful, flirty and even mildly camp, but the undercurrents are bleak as blindness is clearly imminent.

Nevertheless, the pair fire into a fully-blown romantic number, lumberjacks and labourers pirouetting on the open train behind them as Jeff serenades Selma with more vistas she will never glimpse: Niagara Falls, the Empire State Building, her grandson's hand in hers. Selma, for

her part, takes solace in the "infinity in a grain of sand" defence: "I have seen the brightness in one little spark."

Von Trier's direction and a genuinely gripping performance by Björk, all brave resolve and sideways glances, betray that it is clearly an absurdity to imagine that a creature as sensual as Selma can ever be sated with experiences, but still the chorus line of flatbed truck workers add their *basso profundo* support to her deep-in-denial contention, until the dream sequence ends in the manner it began, with Jeff's clumsy, horrified enquiry: "You can't see, can you?"

On *Selmasongs*, unsurprisingly, Radiohead's Thom Yorke proves a far more flexible and expressive duet partner, his dry delivery perfect for a lyric heavy with intimations of mortality and existential dread. In contrast to the Björk-dominated movie number, the lines are carved up more democratically between the pair. In the second verse they reverse the roles, with Björk playing the concerned accuser and Yorke the defensive, evasive victim of failing sight.

Björk, Mendoza and Guy Sigsworth's gorgeouly lavish and elaborate orchestration and arrangements work as a stunning counterpoint to the fearful horror of the subject matter, with the clever wordplay ("Have you seen the Great Wall?/All walls are great if the roof doesn't fall") another potent feature. Björk is also in fantastic form, her anguished vocal soaring as if attempting to escape her flawed physical manifestation.

As the song ends, Björk and Yorke join in repeating the title as if sharing in an act of mutual denial before the track ends, as it began, with the rhythm of the open train creaking down the tracks.

'I've Seen It All' is another Björk/Sjón/Von Trier composition, and it's interesting to note that the director receives co-writing credits for four tracks on *Dancer In The Dark*, despite telling journalists that he had written only two. We can only speculate about the process of back-and-forth between the two headstrong Scandinavians before the soundtrack was finally completed.

OPPOSITE:
Thom Yorke: Björk's vocal partner on 'I've Seen it All' on Selma Songs.

LEFT:
Selma talks with Kathy.

04
Scatterheart

'Scatterheart' is situated in *Dancer In The Dark* at the terrible point at which Selma's fortunes plummet into the Kafka-esque horror sequence that eventually leads to her death.

Arriving home to find she has been robbed of her precious fortune, Selma haltingly confronts Bill about the theft. Wracked with guilt, he still refuses to return the money, and pulls a gun on her. In the desperate struggle that follows, Selma accidentally shoots him in the leg. The errant police officer begs Selma to kill him and, sobbing uncontrollably, she does so, first shooting him repeatedly then, in a scene that has the viewer wincing, crashing a metal case hard on to his head. Von Trier's stark, unflinching realism certainly makes for a grotesque watching experience.

True to her character, Selma then escapes into musical fantasy. A stuck needle on a record in Bill's study sends her into a reverie, from which emerges 'Scatterheart', a song of reconciliation and understanding and the soundtrack to a piece of hugely affecting cinematography. It opens with an almost nursery rhyme quality ("Black night is falling/The sun is gone to bed") which is then both exacerbated and subverted as Selma addresses Bill's battered, bloody corpse as "sleepyhead".

The slain policeman rises to his feet as a hypnotic, powerful electro-beat kicks in and illustrates the dream-like sequence. He washes his face in the bathroom as Selma, flitting around him, asks, "Does it hurt?". Bill, showing the grace and gallantry he profoundly lacked in life, gently reassures her: "I hurt you much more/So don't you worry."

The pair dance a bizarre *pas-de-deux* and converse like conspirators as Bill tells Selma to remain strong and she berates herself for the tragedy that has occurred. Eerily, her son Gene then joins the song, assuring his mother in a shrill soprano that "you just did what you had to do" as he rides his bike in circles in the yard outside the window.

Selma begs, and is granted, forgiveness for Bill's murder as the song ends and police sirens are heard in the distance. He ushers her into the yard, where his wife Linda (Cara Seymour) gives Selma generous encouragement and helps Selma to avoid the police. She sees her son for the last time, and the song ends with Selma dancing and sobbing knee-deep in the dirty stream alongside her home.

Dave Morse, who plays Bill in the movie, is probably the weakest vocalist in *Dancer In The Dark*, and it's no surprise that Björk excised her thespian colleague from the version that appears on *Selmasongs*. Instead, over a twitchy, uncertain pulse-beat she sings a pensive duet with herself, alternating maternal assurance that comfort may be found "in the eye of the hurricane" with a more foreboding, tough love message: "You are gonna have to find out for yourself."

As Björk transfers Selma's mental torment to song, trying to find words to reassure her in her darkest hour, one is reminded of Catherine Deneuve's concern that Björk had suffered too much on Selma's behalf, an impression hardly reduced by one defiant interview comment from the singer: "All through the film, I felt strongly about protecting her, because I thought I knew her pretty well. We got a lot of things in common."

On a lighter note, Lars Von Trier, along with Sjón, scores his third songwriting co-credit here, implying that Björk can't have been as contemptuous toward the Dane's lyrical abilities as he had gloomily imagined.

Björk arrives
at the Cannes
premiere of Dancer
in The Dark.

05 In the Musicals

As *Dancer In The Dark* nears its terrible, grisly conclusion, Björk's character Selma retreats into ever more fantastical and imaginative musical dreamscapes as her fate closes around her.

On trial for Bill's murder, a traumatized Selma retreats into herself in the dock as a barrage of circumstantial evidence, together with her noble refusal to tell the court she was saving money for Gene's illness, combine to make a guilty verdict inevitable. The case against her strengthens when the prosecutor calls as a witness Oldrich Novy (Joel Grey), a veteran Czech tap dancer and Selma's childhood hero.

Selma had told the court, as an innocently whimsical cover story, that she was saving money to send to her sick father in Czechoslovakia, named Oldrich Novy. Naturally, the baffled dancer explodes this fiction. As Selma sits in despair, she hears a rudimentary rhythm in the court artist's scratchy pencil, and another musical fantasy sequence ensues.

In *Dancer In The Dark*, 'In The Musicals' is a duet between Selma and Novy. The doomed girl thanks the veteran performer for all the hours of joy that he gave her as a child and the pair launch into an exuberant dance, Novy even tap-dancing on the judge's bench as the court claps along with indulgent glee. Only the judge rising to pass the death sentence on Selma curtails this poignant escapist interlude.

The track is another Björk/Sjón/Mark Bell/Von Trier composition, and on *Selmasongs* Björk performs the song solo, shifting the emphasis away from her specific love for Novy to a more generalized appreciation of musicals (although it is also easily read as another pledge of consuming, exclusive love for a partner *à la* 'Aeroplane').

The music is a chaotic, explosive yet sleekly structured collision of elements in textbook stage musical style, and Björk's vocal suitably enraptured and appreciative. Like all the tunes in *Dancer In The Dark*, it's a ray of sunshine in a seemingly never-ending, ever-darkening night.

06 107 Steps

One critic reviewing *Dancer In The Dark* commented astutely that Lars Von Trier "simply doesn't know when to quit," and in the sequence of the movie soundtracked by '107 Steps', Von Trier and Björk push the character of Selma to the absolute limit.

Having declined the opportunity of having her death sentence commuted because it may jeopardize Gene's surgery, a distraught and desperate Selma is led to the gallows by Brenda (Siobhan Fallon), a death row warder who has befriended her. The perspicacious Brenda has learnt Selma's key to escaping her terrible fate temporarily, and devises a plan. As the pair walk the infamous 107 steps to the execution scene, Brenda persuades Selma to stamp her feet heavily on the ground, setting off a rhythm that she knows will transport the abject Czech girl into another reverie.

The plan works, and as the guarding warders perform a camp high-step march down the grey corridors, Selma skips from cell to cell comforting fellow convicts, hugging prisoners and waltzing with a warder, all the while singing numbers as she counts off the steps to her demise, Brenda whispering every digit as a macabre backbeat.

Vincent Mendoza's exquisite string arrangement lifts the gloom fleetingly, but as Brenda counts into the nineties and Selma's death beckons, even this passing beauty deepens into a foreboding, crashing portent of doom which finally dissolves into funereal brass and timpani.

On *Selmasongs*, '107 Steps' makes for painful listening precisely because it is impossible to separate the song from the eviscerating movie image of Selma Jezkova marching to her doom, her inner strength and courage in adversity crushed by the inhumane fate awaiting her.

07 New World

Omitting from the album the almost illegally harrowing 'Next To Last Song', sung by Selma with a noose around her neck in the last seconds of her life, Björk chose instead to end *Selmasongs* with

LEFT:
Björk with Catherine Deneuve at Cannes.

'New World', the closing credits song from *Dancer In The Dark*.

The track opens with a warm, bass-friendly electro-hum as, in the movie, the camera pans upward from Selma's swinging corpse into the darkness above the gallows scaffold. Björk's vocal then kicks in, with a lyric echoing the sentiment of 'My Favourite Things', Selma's fave tune from *The Sound Of Music*: "Train whistles, sweet Clementine/ Blueberries, dancers in line."

It feels fatuous to consider the notion of a happy ending to *Dancer In The Dark*, or indeed to any Von Trier movie, but it's not just the 'New World' title (suffixed with 'Overture' in the movie credits) that implies Selma, freed from her dreadful earthly torment, is *en route* to a positive after-life experience. "If living is seeing, I'm holding my breath," Björk chirps: "In wonder, I wonder, what will happen next?"

Idyllic lyrical references to sunlight in her hair and

walking on air further imply that Selma has been rescued by death, but even this striking closing number can't erase from the cinema-goers' mind the tormented scenes they have just witnessed.

Dancer In The Dark was scheduled for a September 2000 release, but a full four months before that the movie's reputation and media profile was upped dramatically. On May 21 at the Cannes film festival in the south of France, the film was awarded the Palme D'Or, the ultimate prize at the ceremony – and Björk picked up the same prize for best actress.

Despite this spectacular accolade, Björk dropped a bombshell at the press conference called the day after she was given the award. After a short and very intense career in the movie world, she was retiring from cinema. "I knew when I said that I would play Selma that it would be both my first and my last role," she told the conference. "I'm happy that this experience would be the one.

OPPOSITE:
**Björk and THAT
swan dress lay
an egg at the
Academy Awards.**

112 Chapter 08

But I have to do music now. I have lost a lot of time. I have only fifty years left and I have to do a lot of records."

The impression that the film world had lost a potential major new talent was borne out when *Dancer In The Dark* went on general release in September. Von Trier's abrasive, uncompromising directorial style split the critics as it invariably did. Björk, however, received almost universal bouquets. Paul Tatara of US media giant CNN typified the media response. Writing on the company's arts website, he said, "Von Trier's achievement is too long-winded and wavering to be completely satisfying. The real reason to see this movie is a remarkable debut performance by the strangely childlike Icelandic pop star Björk. She so fully deserves an Academy Award that they should mail it to her right now and skip the nominations."

Tatara was not alone in his enthusiasm, but Björk's sole Oscar nomination was for the original soundtrack – best song category, for 'I've Seen It All'. Despite giving a spirited reading of the number, clad in her infamous swan dress (Thom Yorke was due to accompany her, but dropped out when the time the song was allotted was cut), she lost out to Bob Dylan's 'Things Have Changed' from *Wonder Boys*.

So would Björk ever change her mind and return to the movie world? Given the striking language she has used to describe her experience in *Dancer In The Dark*, it appears unlikely. There were times, she had explained, when she'd felt like an adulteress. "At some periods I felt like I was having an affair from music, I felt dirty," she divulged. "Because music has always been the place that sorts me out. Everything else can go horribly wrong, but there's always music for me."

And from *Dancer In The Dark*, Björk proceeded to another project with a title evoking the night – but of a different hue entirely.

2000

VESPERTINE

EVER SINCE THE SUGARCUBES BROKE BIG IN 1988, BJÖRK HAD BEEN IN THE PUBLIC EYE. THE MASS FASCINATION INDUCED BY HER MULTI-MILLION SELLER *DEBUT* IN 1993 HAD LIFTED THE ATTENTION TO ANOTHER PLANE, AND THE TURN OF THE MILLENNIUM HAD SEEN CELEBRITY LAY AN EVER BIGGER CLAIM TO HER AFTER HER STARRING TURN IN THE PALME D'OR-WINNING *DANCER IN THE DARK*.

This had frequently been a difficult process for a singer who, despite the flamboyant external eccentricities, remained essentially a shy and self-conscious soul. As 2000 dawned, and as Lars Von Trier continued the post-production work on *Dancer In The Dark*, Björk Gudmundsdóttir returned to Reykjavik in search of privacy.

She also whole-heartedly embraced a radical rethink of the very way in which she composed and created music. Ever the anti-Luddite, Björk had spent her entire solo career to date working on the cutting edge of technology in a way that no other international singing superstar would remotely countenance. For the recording of her new album, she turned to the laptop.

"I've become obsessed with my laptop and my laptop speakers," she confessed to *Wired* magazine at the time. "There's a classical programme called Sibelius, where you have all the instruments of an orchestra in a laptop. You get a picture of sheet music, use a mouse as a pencil, write it out and press 'Play', then print it and hand the music to an orchestra."

Freed from the need to work in a studio, Björk took her laptop to remote corners of Iceland and worked at home as she began to sketch the shape of the new record. She also began to experience an understandable creative reaction against the passionate confessionals of *Homogenic* and the melodramatic theatricality of *Dancer In The Dark*. Björk was ready to make a record all about rediscovering the private self.

When she chatted to fans on her official website in June 2000, a few months into the album, Björk had alighted upon a telling working title for the album: *Domestica*. The record, she explained, was proving to be a reflex reaction to the excesses of *Dancer In The Dark*. "The film was very harsh, quite dark, and emotionally brutal," she said. "So I guess what I'm doing now has a tendency to be the opposite, which I guess is gentle, humorous, happy and kind."

Björk continued to write in Iceland, drafting in Guy Sigsworth once more to help with writing and arranging, as well as spending time at her favoured El Cortijo studio in San Pedro, Spain. The summer saw her fly to New York, where she spent many weeks working in a loft space with Zeena Parkins, an avant-garde harpist with a fascinating resumé.

Parkins had written numerous scores for theatre, dance and film productions, as well as collaborating with such like-minded musical souls as John Zorn and Sonic Youth's Thurston Moore. She had even, remarkably, played with Courtney Love's band Hole on their *MTV Unplugged* recording. Björk was most interested, however, by Parkins' pioneering work in applying digital processing to the harp.

"I want to use the noises that everybody is using every day," Björk told journalist David Toop, reprising a familiar theme. "The remote control, the

mobile phone, the Internet, the fax machine. It's not weird or avant-garde to do that. Digital stuff is all around us anyway, so why not make a song out of it?"

While in New York, Björk also met performance artist Matthew Barney, the man who was to prove the most lasting and serious of the string of relationships she had entered into in recent years. If Perkins was to help shape the musical vibe of the album, Barney had an equal influence on its lyrical and emotional content.

As autumn fell, Björk returned to Iceland for a further recording session with long-time collaborator Marius de Vries and Protools recording engineer Jake Davies, interrupted only by promotional duties for the just-released *Dancer In The Dark*. At this relatively late stage in the day, Björk also introduced an utterly new factor into the equation: San Francisco-based electronic experimentalists Matmos.

Matmos, who comprised duo Andrew Daniel and Martin "MC" Schmidt, had released their eponymous debut album in 1997. Its rigorous dissections of found noises such as amplified crayfish nerve tissue, freshly cut hair, the pages of Bibles turning and a frozen stream thawing in the sun had led to a limited degree of interest from devotees of UK techno avant-gardists such as Autechre and The Aphex Twin.

Björk had first contacted Matmos when they remixed 'Alarm Call' from *Homogenic*. She'd arrived from totally out of their orbit. "We'd never met her in our life," confessed Schmidt. "We didn't even own any of her records."

Björk sent Matmos files of the album in progress, with the request to add their slant to proceedings. Matmos were surprised by the request, but intrigued by the challenge. 'We'd never dealt with a vocal or with something that had that verse-chorus structure, so it was really strange for us," reflected Daniel.

Nevertheless, Matmos contributed their maverick input, and the album was finally completed by Christmas 2000, although a further eight months were to pass before it was released.

There had also been one further change along the way. No longer *Domestica*, Björk's new album was now to be named *Vespertine*: a word meaning, variously, pertaining to the evening, the opening of a flower, or the time near sunset. Or, of course,

Björk's swan dress was to prove the visual metaphor for Vespertine.

01 Hidden Place

Sharp and sensual yet heavy with nuance, the delicious 'Hidden Place' was a perfect introduction to the intimate delights of *Vespertine*, both musically and lyrically. "Through the warmest chord of care/Your love was sent to me," Björk breathes as the song opens, the very same phrase she used in her sleeve notes when dedicating *Vespertine* to her Manhattan-based new lover, Matthew Barney. It's immediately evident that 'Hidden Place' is a song about an emergent, fledgling new relationship, a love as yet too timid to speak its name.

The sentiment of "I have been completely shy/But I can almost smell a pinch of hope" is an almost direct echo of "Your flirt finds me out" from 'Possibly Maybe', written when Björk was on the verge of her affair with Stephane Sednaoui. Björk has always had a fondness, and a talent, for chronicling the tender, doubt-laden early stages of love, and 'Hidden Place' finds her longing to drag her would-be *amour* to a secluded spot to test and enjoy their reactions to each other.

Unlike 'Possibly Maybe', this isn't a stormy, doomed relationship to be played out and spent within the course of a song. Björk worries that she should maybe be "careful" and hide her love "under a blanket", but as the song proceeds she can't stop herself lauding her "beautifullest, fragilest" new partner.

"'Hidden Place' is about how two people can create a paradise just by uniting," Björk told *CDNow*. "You've got an emotional location that's mutual, and it's unbreakable."

Musically, 'Hidden Place' functions around some brooding, deliciously equivocal programing by Guy Sigsworth together with Matthew Herbert, the *enfant terrible* of the UK *musique concrete* scene. Björk provides a pulse-like bassline and Vincent Mendoza, a musical partner-in-crime from *Dancer In The Dark*, oversees a reliably sweeping string arrangement through which chorus the voices of an electronically treated, celestial-sounding choir.

evening prayers: Björk had sung much of the album at twilight, in Iceland, walking alone by the ocean.

Where *Homogenic* had often been harsh and abrasive, *Vespertine* was warm and yielding. Intimate, introverted and revelling in sonic possibility, this was the sensual musical exploration of self that Björk had been longing to make, left to her own devices, ever since she was launched into the public eye over a decade earlier.

"I needed this album to explore what we sound like on the inside," Björk explained, brilliantly, to one enquiring writer. "It's that ecstasy, that euphoric state that happens when whispering. It's very much about being alone in your house, in a very quiet sort of introverted mood."

Wrapped in a monochrome sleeve showing Björk wearing the very swan dress that had caused such a stir at that year's Oscars, *Vespertine* was finally released at the end of August 2001. By the sound of it, Björk's house was now a happy place to be.

Matmos also receive a programming credit on 'Hidden Place' but some critics struggled to find their signature sound on *Vespertine*, and the duo themselves freely admitted that they were unable to exercise much influence. "The casual listener may be hard-pressed to find any Matmos," admitted Martin Schmidt to the *Pitchfork* webzine. "When Björk asked us to work on *Vespertine*, it was eighty per cent completed. We were sent recordings with a full orchestra and a full choir and asked to add to them! So [our contribution] does sound like a little bit, piled up on top of a big pile …"

'Hidden Place' was released as a single in the UK in August 2001 and reached number 21 in the chart.

02 Cocoon

In most people's eyes the stand-out track from *Vespertine*, 'Cocoon' was the most literal, obvious realization of Björk's musical philosophy for this particular album.

"For the first time in my life, I wanted to create a paradise on this album," Björk said, around the time of *Vespertine*'s release. "This record is all about making a cocoon, a paradise to escape to. You couldn't take this cocoon anywhere, but you still believe in the right for it to exist."

'Cocoon' is another song about retiring from the world to perfect seclusion with a loving soulmate, but the affair has moved on apace from the hesitation of 'Hidden Place'. By now intimately entwined with Matthew Barney, Björk marvels at the tenderness and steadfastness he brings to their emotional and sexual relationship. It is, she trills, "a beauty this immense" and "a saintly trance".

Björk's plucky attempts to capture the intangible, ethereal nature of profound love are endearing, as is her characteristic unique candidness as she describes their physical union: "He slides inside/Half awake, half asleep." The pair sleep, sexually conjoined, until Björk awakes in his arms to discover: "Gorgeousness! He's still inside me!"

'Cocoon' closes with an extravagant and somewhat unusual metaphor for the act of love, as Björk describes "a train of pearls, cabin by cabin" being shot across an ocean. It's an interesting variant on the old trains-into-tunnels routine, and the kindest response is probably to applaud the ambitious imagination behind the simile.

Björk co-wrote 'Cocoon' with Thomas Knak, a left-field electronic musician who records under the names Opiate and Future 3. Having met him in Copenhagen while completing filming on *Dancer In The Dark*, she invited Knak to Iceland in late January 2000. "He makes gorgeous music," she said, simply. "He was definitely the most pleasant surprise about Denmark."

Between them, Björk and Knak dream up a beauteous, scarcely-there backing track over which Björk whispers in a vocal so credulous and love-laden that it seems to enter the realm of the abstract. Simon Reynolds of the *New York Times*

compared *Vespertine*'s "glitch-pop" to the "jackfrost wonderland" of UK icons of the 1980s, the Cocteau Twins, a perfect comparison for the blissed-out electro-pop of 'Cocoon'.

03
It's Not Up To You

Continuing the benign soul-searching of *Vespertine*, 'It's Not Up To You' finds Björk undertaking a wry dialogue with herself about the random nature of everyday life.

"I wake up/and the day feels broken," she opens, before taking off on a gently self-mocking soliloquy on how the situation can be redressed: "How do I master the perfect day?/Six glasses of water, seven phone calls."

Björk may have famously declared "I'm no fucking Buddhist!" on *Homogenic*'s 'Alarm Call', but there's a decidedly Zen quality to her assertion on 'It's Not Up To You' that anybody suffering a

bad day should go with its energy, rather than trying to fight it: "Just lean into the crack." As she chirrups into the chorus, Björk playfully scolds herself for thinking she is capable of guiding the hand of random fate. Surrendering joyously to the inevitability of life's chance events, rather than trying to fight them, is a regular Björk lyrical undertow, and one she explained in typically tangential fashion around the release of *Vespertine*.

"Your grandmother calls because she's sick, but you put on a lipstick because you're going out to meet your boyfriend," she said, sketching a typical happenstance day. "You meet a dog that's thrown up on the way. You have to juggle all those things and make them work. If it's a good day you have a good juggle, then you have some days that are crap and you just can't."

'It's Not Up To You' is awash in vast, luscious instrumentation, with harp and clavichord to the fore of a Powerbook symphony. It also boasts one of the best tunes on the album, a commodity that a few nay-sayers hinted was in rather short supply. The treated electro-cherubic choir, though, is once again the *coup de grace*.

04 Undo

'Undo' continues where 'It's Not Up To You' leaves off, being another quasi-Taoist exhortation to an unnamed soul to give in to destiny and not resist fate. Anybody tuning only to these two songs from *Vespertine* could be forgiven for assuming that Björk had, as she pondered years ago in 'Possibly Maybe', "joined a cult".

If 'Undo' is lyrically a re-tread of its predecessor, being full of urgings to "lean in to it" and "surrender", musically it has far more in common with 'Cocoon'. 'Undo' is Björk's second co-composition with Thomas Knak, and it shares the halting, wondrous yet somehow serene ambience of 'Cocoon'. The vibe is, as Björk breathes toward the end of the measured joy, "quietly ecstatic".

LEFT:
Siouxie and the Banshees: early post-punk icons of the 1980s evoked by 'Pagan Poetry'.

05 Pagan Poetry

Fulsome and brooding, the electro-treatise of 'Pagan Poetry' is yet another take on what is probably Björk's most consistent lyrical obsession – the peculiar, singular attraction that compels a human to take a specific fellow creature as a partner.

Unusually for Björk, who usually favours a lyrical directness that can occasionally be endearingly gauche, 'Pagan Poetry' is couched in elaborate, almost ritualistic language, and decidedly over-written. "Pedalling through the dark currents," she recites ominously, "I find an accurate copy, a blueprint/Of the pleasure in me." It seems a somewhat arcane way to communicate that she fancies someone.

Moving through a mannered handshake intro-duction and an odd image of swirling, ripe black lilies, Björk muses on dark, primal attractions beneath the surface that make lovers recognize each other via secret codes and signals. The impli-

cation is that humans are not in control: greater forces are weaving these spells.

'Pagan Poetry' is an alluring semi-Gothic lament that had some critics recalling the sleek sheen of post-punk icons Siouxsie & The Banshees and, particularly, their 1982 album *A Kiss In The Dreamhouse*. The impression was reinforced by the strong contribution of Zeena Parkins and also Björk's glass music box, both reminiscent of the Banshees' (at the time) laudably exotic instrumentation.

The aloof Siouxsie, though, would never have dared or deigned to pull the trick that Björk does at the end of 'Pagan Poetry'. As the spiralling techno-storm descends into silence, she pledges her love and passions naked to the world: "I love him, I love him, I love him." As if in vindication, a choir of sampled Björks repeat her devotion back to her: "She loves him, she loves him, she loves him." It's a quirky and quixotic device and, in its audacious frankness, highly compelling.

06 Frosti

An instrumental that weighs in at a mere one minute forty-five seconds, 'Frosti' is both the shortest and – on first hearing – least conse-quential number on *Vespertine*, but its pristine gleam and fairyland prettiness soon alter that perception. Played on the ornate, beautifully sculpted glass music box that Björk proudly carried on tour with her around the globe, it suggests the twinkling soundtrack to a twilight evening snowfall – is the name 'Frosti' mere coincidence?

Björkophiles are likely to be put in mind of 'My Spine', the *Telegram* trifle that Björk dreamt up with percussionist Evelyn Glennie, but 'Frosti' works simply because it is, in Björk's own much-favoured phrase, "gorgeous" right until the moment that it segues into the somewhat more portentous follow-ing track.

07 Aurora

Rapt, serene, yet alive with desire, 'Aurora' finds Björk, at sunrise, treading softly across Icelandic glaciers in search of the northern lights.

Fading in from the fairy grotto twinkle of 'Frosti', 'Aurora' begins with Matmos mimicking the snap and crackle of feet trudging through deep snow (an effect they reproduced live by the somewhat prosaic means of stamping on a box of gravel). Björk then looms in, her radiant vocal acquiring a spectral hue as she observes the Arctic's famed unearthly glow: "Looking hard for moments of shine."

Addressing Aurora, the Roman goddess of the dawn, Björk begs for permission to leave the Earth and be part of the sublime night sky spectacle: "Shoot me beyond this suffer/The need is great." Her imagination aflame, she hallucinates that she glimpses the pagan deity in a shadow, then fills her mouth with snow, the greater to appreciate the beauty and natural wonder of the moment.

Zeena Parkins' shimmering harp and Björk's delicate, chiming music box again evoke a poised, primitive beauty as the song ends with Björk apparently reverting to a tribal chant as she beseeches Aurora to bring a new day: "Spark the sun off."

08
An Echo, A Stain

Obsessive and carefully spooky, 'An Echo, A Stain' is a track that could easily have soundtracked one of Selma's more chilling late dream sequences in *Dancer In The Dark*.

One of the more enigmatic excursions on *Vespertine*, the exact subject matter of 'An Echo, A Stain' is uncertain – has Björk, perhaps, dreamt a near-death experience? The haunting lyric "Feel my breath on your neck/And your heart will race", combined with the assured promise to rendezvous "soon", seem to imply that she has encountered a Grim Reaper-type figure. Spared, Björk knows that inevitably they will meet again.

It should be noted that such ambiguity is traditionally a rarity in Björk's lyrics, where linear narrative and heartfelt passion tend to rule, but 'An Echo, A Stain' is typical of the tendency in *Vespertine* to float into the linguistic realm of metaphor and abstraction.

When Björk croons "I'm sorry you saw that/I'm sorry he did it" there are echoes of the non-specific relationship crimes of *Post*'s "You've Been Flirting Again", but 'An Echo, A Stain' breathes far more rarefied air; as *Rolling Stone* noted, "Björk's cries and purrs are magnified with such reverbed clarity that she even seems to breathe in melody."

09
Sun In
My Mouth

Like 'An Echo, A Stain', 'Sun In My Mouth' is a co-composition between Björk and her long-time cohort Guy Sigsworth, but this charming chime of harp, celeste and meticulous programing takes its cue from an E.E. Cummings poem, 'Impressions'.

Cummings (1894–1962) experimented radically with form, syntax and punctuation, and was primarily known for writing exclusively in lower case. A playful poet, his preferred subject matters were the transient nature of love and sex and also the futility of war, which he had experienced first-hand as an ambulance driver in France during the First World War.

Björk had never been a great reader: "Even bad music interests me, but with literature I pick fewer things," she admitted to *Life* in late 2001. "For the last three years it's been Cummings for me, though. Not the politics or the satire, but the love and pretty things."

'Sun In My Mouth' opens with the last two lines of 'Impressions' from Cummings' 1922 collection *Tulips & Chimneys* then becomes a celebration of sensory overload, Björk recalling the cliff-top plunge of *Post*'s 'Hyper-ballad' with her desire to leap into the air "with closed eyes/To dash against darkness."

Fragile and immaculate, the string-powered 'Sun In My Mouth' is sweet synthetic digitalia of the kind that *Vespertine* possesses in abundance, although Björk's new-found affec-

tion for lyrical complexity left many fans scratching their heads as they attempted to decipher the "chasteness of seagulls".

Björk's co-writer Sigsworth, meanwhile, used the opportunity of the release of *Vespertine* to pay tribute to the star with whom he'd now worked for the best part of a decade. "I think Björk really is one of the great voices of now," he avowed. "In years to come, people will look on her with the kind of reverence they afford Billie Holiday or Ella Fitzgerald. There's just that special kind of … uniqueness in her voice."

10 Heirloom

'Heirloom', by far the most uptempo track on *Vespertine*, was a co-composition between Björk and Martin Gretschmann, a Bavarian who for musical purposes adopts the name of his one-man electronica project, Console.

Both solo and as part of hip noiseniks The Notwist, Console's speciality is a clever sonic collage that utilizes 1980s musical equipment such as Casio organs. The critic Ryan Schreiber noted that 'Heirloom' opens as if somebody had "pre-set samba on a vintage Wurlitzer organ." Conventional keyboards would maybe sound simply too jarring here.

In the context of *Vespertine*, Björk's relatively chirpy vocal on this song sounds positively raucous as she recites a whimsical dream in which every time she loses her voice, her mother and son bake "little glowing lights" for her to eat. Quite what Freud would make of it is anybody's guess.

As Björk's peculiar take on lyrical psychedelia comes to an end, Console fires a chorus of Björks back at her, layering her voice into a choir just as Björk had done earlier on 'Pagan Poetry'. A late addition to *Vespertine*, 'Heirloom' left many fans wishing that Björk had followed her original instinct to omit the track.

11 Harm of Will

'Harm Of Will' features easily the oddest collaboration on *Vespertine*, finding Björk singing some notably bizarre lyrics by gifted but troubled US movie writer and director Harmony Korine.

Korine became notorious while still in his teens when he wrote the script and screenplay for Larry Clark's nihilistic, amoral take on US slacker youth, *Kids*. In 1999, he both wrote and directed *Julien Donkey-Boy*, the disturbing yet fascinating tale of a schizophrenic working with blind children who commits acts of random violence. Korine also signed the Dogma declaration of cinematic purity together with Lars Von Trier, through whom he met Björk.

Korine's lyric for 'Harm Of Will' loosely sketches a troubadour and libertine who takes commitment-free sexual pleasure from his conquests and includes a reference to oral sex, although this is unlikely to faze a singer who has, on *Vespertine*, already described awaking to discover her sleeping lover's penis inside her.

Björk unravels Korine's words with tremulous diligence over another Guy Sigsworth-style string and electronica arrangement, abetted by gloriously sympathetic orchestration by Vincent Mendoza, and her serene delivery somehow renders the would-be freakish narrative unremarkable – or, rather, simply overpowers it.

12 Unison

Alive with humour and self-knowledge and boasting a glorious, soaring melody line, 'Unison' was a fitting climax to *Vespertine*, Björk's most poised and precious album to date by quite some length.

Opening with the acappella assertion that "one hand loves the other so much on me," 'Unison' quickly develops into a delicious, defiant defence by Björk of her singular life philosophy. Admitting to being "born stubborn, me," she goes on to predict that she will always follow her own peculiar, singular (Northern?) lights.

There is much gentle, gracious charm, and the image of a hermit-Björk with beard, pipe and parrot is one to conjure with. The song would be mere 'Heirloom'-style irritant whimsy, though, were it not for a lavish, breathtaking melody dreamt up by Björk and her army of five fellow co-programmers.

The celestial choir hove into view again, and Björk also makes use of a sample from a song called 'Aero Deck' by German electro-experimentalist Markus Popp, aka Oval, who is known for scratching CDs in order to record the consequent random rhythmic clicking. There are moments of doubt – "I never thought I would compromise" – but Björk ends the album in positive mode, beckoning her lover "Let's unite tonight."

Released in August 2001 to near universal adulatory reviews, *Vespertine* entered the UK chart at number 8 and topped the album charts in France, Spain and Norway. It also entered the US *Billboard* chart at number 19 – Björk's highest ever position in the States.

1990

SINGLES, B-SIDES AND SIDE PROJECTS

01 Amphibian
02 Batabid
03 Charlene
04 Domestica
05 Foot Soldier
06 Generous Palmstroke
07 Glóra
08 I Go Humble
09 I Remember You
10 Karvel
11 Mother Heroic
12 My Snare
13 Next To Last Song
14 Ooops
15 Play Dead
16 Qmart
17 Scary
18 Short Term Affair
19 Sidasta Ég
20 So Broken
21 Sod Off
22 Stigdu Mig
23 Sweet Intuition
24 Verandi
25 Visur Vatnsenda-Rosu

01
Amphibian

Spike Jonze shot the award-winning, attention-grabbing video for 'It's Oh So Quiet' that brought Björk to the attention of Lars Von Trier and led to the role of Selma in *Dancer In The Dark*, and Björk returned the favour by contributing 'Amphibian' to the soundtrack of Jonze's critical and box office hit *Being John Malkovich*. It was also released as a B-side to 'Cocoon'.

Sung entirely in Icelandic, 'Amphibian' is an amorphous, evocative piece that Björk croons in distracted fashion over a click track-style drum pattern and transient, slight harp accompaniment while somebody unknown whistles in the background. Björk, Mark Bell and Valgeir Sigurdsson's production feeds separate Björk vocals and lyrics through left and right speakers, as though she is engaged in a dreamy internal dialogue with herself, and the vibe is positively oceanic.

02 Batabid

That extreme rarity, a Björk instrumental, 'Batabid' is a 2-minute 26-second filler on a CD-single version of 'Pagan Poetry' that finds Björk, abetted by Mark Bell, unleashing a lovely, aquatic-sounding electronic treatment that sails majestically around its allotted space as gracefully as the swans that represent the visual metaphor for Björk's *Vespertine* period. It's sweet, sensual, and over as soon as it's begun.

03 Charlene

Written by Björk with three-man UK techno avant-gardists Black Dog, 'Charlene' was a Björk/Nellee Hooper co-production from the Bahamas *Post* sessions that finished up as a B-side to the 'Isobel' single. Opening with a gurgle of running water, 'Charlene' is a fun, evocative sliver of

Over a loping, easily-paced techno-squiggle, Björk exults in the naughty-girls together ambience of the ditty, and it's hard to agree with the hyperventilating critic who, tongue lolling, located 'lesbian sex undercurrents' in Björk's invitation to 'dry' the friend with whom she is 'naked and laughing'. Nevertheless, 'Charlene' is a great electro-pop song from a highly fertile and creative period in Björk's history.

04 Domestica

Domestica was the working title of *Vespertine* for a large part of that album's creation, which would imply that this busy, clattering track was intended to figure on it. The song finds Björk whole-heartedly embracing the magic realism and bliss in the mundane that was her declared aim coming out of *Dancer In The Dark*: the cutesy, eyes-to-heaven theme of losing her house keys as a taxi awaits outside seems almost comically banal, but Valgier Sigurdsson's programing input helps to make this contented, cosy little track a plausible snippet. 'Domestica' finally appeared as an extra track on a 'Pagan Poetry' single.

05 Foot Soldier

'Foot Soldier' is a dainty yet darkly preoccupied joint venture between Björk and Mark Bell that had its genesis in the *Vespertine* sessions and came to light as a backing track to 'Hidden Place'. Bell's watchful, brooding programing conjures up an air of oddly disturbing menace as Björk gives full voice to a lyric that revisits territory first touched upon by, among others, 'Cover Me' from *Post* or *Homogenic*'s 'Hunter'. Usually at the head of the mission, this time Björk instead urges a mysterious, unidentified foot soldier to leap adventurously into the dark and boldly go where danger may lie, even as Bell's fractured beats make the prospect sound a highly unenticing one.

electro-pop that finds Björk pledging love and sisterly devotion to a reckless, mischievous friend with whom she is skinny-dipping. Björk generally acquaints the ocean with freedom and escape from constricting etiquette, as previously witnessed on *Debut*'s 'The Anchor Song' and the boat-stealing late-night harbour antics of 'There's More To Life Than This'.

06 Generous Palmstroke

The sharp, incisive 'Generous Palmstroke' figured on the track listing of *Vespertine* until the very final stages of recording the album, when it was bumped off in favour of the inferior 'Heirloom'. It eventually finished up as a B-side on 'Hidden Place', the first single off the album.

Co-written by Björk and New York-based harpist Zeena Parkins, 'Generous Palmstroke' is given a medieval madrigal feel by Parkins' lusty playing, while Björk's crystal-clear enunciation is precise and diamond-hard. Lyrically, the song is another paean to the newfound love Björk has located with Matthew Barney, as she quaintly reflects that she is better when united with him: "On my own I'm human/I do faults.''

The lyric takes the form of a candid appeal from Björk to her lover to accept her as a soulmate, albeit a "needy" and "raw" one, and realize that she is his for eternity. Even by Björk's standards, the direct-ness and candidness are striking. The song ends with the device, much favoured on *Vespertine*, of a chorus of Björks singing her words back to her.

07 Glóra

Appearing only as a B-side on a CD single fronted by 'Big Time Sensuality', 'Glóra' – Icelandic for "glowing one" – is a Björk flute instrumental of the kind she hadn't released since 'Jóhannes Kjarvalv' on her 1977 kiddie album, and is a slight party piece likely to be of interest only to the most diehard completists.

08 I Go Humble

'I Go Humble' was recorded during the Nellee Hooper-overseen *Post* sessions in Nassau, and it's a tribute to the extraordinary wealth of material that emerged from those sessions that the song failed to make the cut on to the album, eventually coming to light as a support track on the 'Isobel' single.

A co-composition between Björk and LFO man Mark Bell, 'I Go Humble' is a jubilant, jaunty electro-doodle over which Björk tells of feelings of unaccustomed humility in the presence of some unknown hero figure. It's unclear whether the song is addressed to a lover or musical colleague, but Björk's admiration is not in doubt: "You're so curiously pure, you amaze me."

As ever with Björk, the occasionally over-literal, English-as-a-second-language line grates ("I'm queen of provocation") but the tongue-in-cheek humour ensures that, as is par for the course, she gets away with it. Björk, Bell and Hooper also combine to ensure this is one of Björk's danciest, more infectious floor-fillers.

09
I Remember You

A backing track on the 'Venus As A Boy' single, 'I Remember You' is a cover of an old standard originally written for the 1930s musical *The Fleet's In* by US film scorer and orchestra leader Victor Schertzinger and his sometime musical partner John H. Mercer. Björk croons through the number accompanied only by veteran harpist Corky Hale, a contributor to *Debut*. This mellow, romantic tune has also been sung over the years by the Beatles, Dinah Washington and Bette Midler, but is most closely associated with yodelling MOR folk/country star Slim Whitman.

10 Karvel

A co-composition with Graham Massey, 'Karvel' dates from Björk's sessions with the 808 State technomeister around the time of *Debut* and *Post*, and finally found its way on to a four-track CD single headed by 'I Miss You'. Over a rolling, fluid Massey electro-rhythm, Björk growls and cajoles a stream-of-consciousness selection of thoughts that recommend ignoring bad advice, never trusting nuns, and loving the whole of humankind. It's a problematic lyric to interpret, but reads most convincingly as a trademark Björkian homily in favour of instinctive and intuitive living as compared to the aridity of an overly mannered existence.

11 Mother Heroic

A product of the *Vespertine* sessions, 'Mother Heroic' was a backing track for a CD single version of 'Hidden Place'. Like 'Sun In My Mouth', which made it on to the album, the track finds Björk and Guy Sigsworth indulging her love of early-twentieth-century American envelope-pushing poet E.E. Cummings. Over Sigsworth's carefully plucked, brittle celeste, Björk recites lines from 'Belgium', Cummings' wordy pledge of devotion to, one presumes, Mary, mother of Christ. Björk has never been known for her love of organized religion, and 'Mother Heroic' works equally well as a general endorsement of self-sacrificing, beatific mother figures.

Singles,
B-sides and
side projects

133

12 My Snare

Jointly written with LFO's Mark Bell yet passed over for *Homogenic*, 'My Snare' – which is also known as 'Nature Is Ancient' – formed a backing track to 'Bachelorette', the most successful single off the album.

Musically and lyrically, 'My Snare' treads familiar Björk terrain. At the time of *Homogenic* she was on a musical mission to recreate in sound the potent landscapes of her native Iceland, and Bell duly supplies a bubbling, erupting techno soundtrack redolent of lava escaping from active geysers. Björk supports this effort with a lyric earnestly lauding the power of the unfettered elements, although her best line in the song is the first one: "It's soft in the middle with a shell around it, it's called life."

Throwing in her mandatory exhortation against

logic and "level-head-ness", Björk closes the track with the stark and vivid image of nature as a personalized, feminized entity with "dark hair on her head" and "blood on her arms", both a sensual creature and one to be feared and respected.

13 Next To Last Song

Perplexingly and inexplicably omitted from *Selmasongs*, 'Next To Last Song' is the draining, profoundly moving song that Björk (as Selma) delivers from the gallows in *Dancer in the Dark* as she prepares to be hung. Having just learnt that her son Gene has successfully undergone his eye operation, the now-blind Selma caresses his glasses in her hand as, acappella, she addresses her song to him: "Dear Gene, of course you are near." It is the only song in the movie that's not a fantasy sequence triggered by everyday noises, and Selma uses the song wryly to bemoan the silence: "The choir is silent/And no-one takes a spin." In a horribly harsh cinematic moment, Lars Von Trier has the gallows trapdoor open under Selma as she croons the song's last words: "And that's all."

14 Ooops

'Ooops' was the first fruit of Björk's collaboration with Manchester acid house band 808 State in 1991, and appeared on the band's *Ex:El* album the same year. Having contacted the band anonymously and enjoyed a successful first meeting, Björk was summoned to Manchester as 808 were recording *Ex:El*, their second album proper, and given two tapes of instrumentals the band had recorded. Björk vanished into the rain with her headphones in search of ideas, returning an hour later to record her vocal.

"I've never seen anybody quite so physical as when Björk records," Graham Massey later told the

New Musical Express. "There's a lot of jumping about, as she is on stage, and if you isolate the microphone, you can hear footstomping noise.'"

Lyrically, 'Ooops' is one of Björk's more extraordinary concoctions. The song opens with her trilling that she'll go to someone's house and "pour myself over you", indulging them and showing them a good time, only to turn suddenly: "Dog, I own you/Sit down fool, you own me."

808 State's trademark heavy, dramatic beats provide a perfect playground for Björk to utilize her repertoire of squeals, cries and whispers, although the nicely downbeat guitar recalls fellow Mancunians New Order (their singer, Bernard Sumner, also guested on *Ex:El*). There's even a slight flamenco tinge to 'Ooops' and it's arguable that the track, in opening Björk's eyes to her potential in dance music, sounded the death knell for the already-ailing Sugarcubes.

Credited to 808 State featuring Björk, 'Ooops' was released as a British single in April 1991, charting at an unspectacular number 42.

15 Play Dead

Written as the theme tune to the Danny Cannon-directed movie *Young Americans*, 'Play Dead' was released as a single in October 1993, while Björk was touring the *Debut* album, and became her biggest hit to date when it reached number 12 in the British chart.

Composer David Arnold had spent years writing soundtracks for his friend Cannon's UK television programmes and documentaries before being asked to provide the theme to *Young Americans*, a movie about modern London starring Harvey Keitel. Desirous of a female voice for the opening and closing credits, Arnold knew instantly where to turn.

"Listening to early Sugarcubes records, everything I heard in my head came out of Björk's mouth," Arnold told Martin Aston in *Björkgraphy*. "I could see the potential in doing something unique with her."

In an interesting precursor to her method-acting approach to playing Selma in *Dancer In The Dark*, Björk asked Cannon to provide a list of primary

emotions in the make-up of the character she was to portray in song, explaining that she would find it hard to produce emotionally wracked songs as she was at the time "very happy".

With the assistance of former PiL bassist and dub warrior Jah Wobble, Arnold and Björk produced an opulent, lavish orchestral score to match Björk's melodramatic words of playing dead to "stop the hurting". Arnold later reported that he was overwhelmed in the recording studio when Björk began to interpret his work via musical ad libbing in Icelandic.

"It was a goose bump moment, and the combination of her voice and the orchestra sounded completely natural," he said. "I thought to myself, 'I can't believe no-one has done this with her before,' and I was glad to be there first."

As *Debut* continued to fly out of the stores in late 1993 and early 1994, 'Play Dead' was added to the album as a bonus twelfth track. Any fans who complained at having bought the first pressings of the album, minus the Arnold/Björk track, were sent a copy of the augmented record free of charge as compensation.

'Play Dead' was released an a single in the UK in October 1993 and became Björk's biggest hit to date, reaching number 12.

16 Qmart

'Qmart' is the more low-key of the two tracks that Björk recorded with 808 State in 1991 that ended up on the Manchester band's *Ex:El* album. Her contribution to the humming, mellow comedown vibe is a series of murmurs, exhalations and yodels that function as one more instrument rather than imposing a narrative on the quietly bubbling, effervescent song dynamic. An exquisite, myriad confection, 'Qmart' is the sort of ambient techno that Björk and Graham Massey later posted to each other and then celebrated on the track 'Headphones' on *Post*.

17 Scary

Written with Guy Sigsworth, who also provides the busy, brittle main harpsichord riff, 'Scary' dates from the *Homogenic* sessions and is vastly similar in tone to 'Five Years', the vitriolic track aimed at Björk's ex-lover Goldie.

It's impossible to specify whether 'Scary' details the failings of Goldie or of Tricky, with whom Björk also enjoyed a short fling around the time of *Homogenic*, but there are lyrical clues that the Bristolian may have been Björk's target. Notoriously unreliable and unpunctual, Tricky is arguably the more likely to inhabit the "dark and spiky" home described in the song, and "heaven and hell" is very likely a reference to 'Hell Is Around The Corner', a landmark Tricky track of the time.

Nevertheless, Sigsworth's perky, madrigal rhythms give the song a decidedly upbeat tone, and Björk appears to be looking back and shaking her head in confused scorn at her men's failings rather than wallowing in the despair of 'Five Years'.

18 Short Term Affair

This fairly ill-advised comedic number was a duet between Björk and comedian Steve Coogan, recorded in 1997 originally for a BBC TV *Comic Relief* charity appeal. Björk had gone on record as being a big fan of Coogan and his comic creation Alan Partridge, a bombastic and clueless regional television presenter with ideas above his station. At the time of *Comic Relief*, Coogan was developing a new character named Tony Ferrino, a Tom Jones/Englebert Humperdinck-style chauvinistic 1970s-style crooner. The character never took off and Ferrino's album, *Phenomenon*, on which this duet appeared, sank without trace.

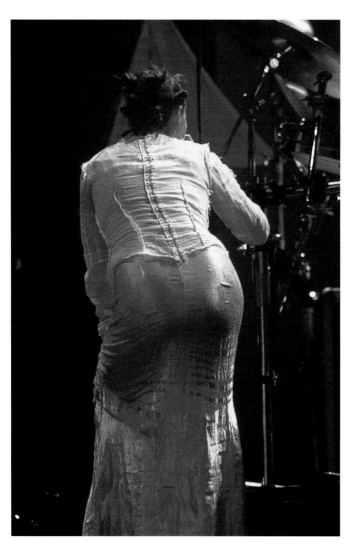

20 So Broken

Feasibly the most emotionally abject track Björk has ever recorded, 'So Broken' is a sorry lament to the end of her relationship with Goldie dating from the *Homogenic* sessions, and finds Björk deep in the pit of despair: "I'm so broken … completely unhealable." Her lyric constantly shifts into Icelandic, as though her adopted second tongue of English is simply incapable of expressing her basest, most heartfelt hurt, and the "heartbreak train" has clearly hit this particular victim hard. This stark confessional appeared as a final track on the 'Jóga' CD single.

21 Sod Off

A warning to a relationship partner on the verge of over-stepping boundaries of emotional decency and mutual respect, 'Sod Off' sees Björk firing another broadside across the bows of her potentially errant lover. The warning that she will not allow the careless culprit to pull her down to his "third-class communication" is icily enunciated, and its inclusion next to the distraught "So Broken" made the four-track "Jóga" CD probably the most wracked mini-set of songs that Björk has ever released.

19 Sídasta Ég

Released as a backing track on 'Big Time Sensuality', 'Sídasta Ég' or 'The Final Me' was a joint composition between Björk, her former husband and Sugarcube Thór Eldon, and Gulli Óttarson, who had been the driving force and band leader of Kukl. Hauntingly intoned in Icelandic by Björk over Óttarson's piecemeal guitar, the sketchy, enigmatic words evoke a sense of loss, or a love gone wrong: Björk begins the song watching "how you move/behind the wallpaper" and then goes "in search of rain", the kind of adolescent poetry that marked Tappi Tíkarrass and Kukl.

22 Stigdu Mig

Released as a backing song on the 'Venus As A Boy' single, 'Stigdu Mir' or 'Step Me' was like 'Sídasta Ég' a Björk/Óttarson/Eldon composition. It's a short, intense number wherein Björk croons over Óttarson's piquant, picked guitar her desire to be 'stepped' to a nature where houses "roll out of fog" and "yellow eyes die". This minimalist, fairly sombre undertaking reminds you exactly why Kukl were frequently compared to Brit post-punk New Wavers like Siouxsie & The Banshees and X-Ray Spex.

expectant whisper/ shriek, Björk gives voice to a state of arousal involving *billets-doux* in, bizarrely, the tummy, and kisses waiting to be unleashed from the mouth, before chastizing herself to take it easy: "Kyrr!"

Over a portentuous, lugubrious string arrangement and a veritable Protools symphony, not to mention Wagnerian operatic accompaniment, Björk struggles to control her stirring passion and "sea of desire" before acknowledging her primal lust to be all about "too much space between the legs." Measured and meticulous, the track climaxes with a sensual string arrangement by Jolly Mukherjee then a drawn-out electro-sigh that slows to a grinding close as if the equipment's plug has been pulled out.

23 Sweet Intuition

This solo Björk composition appeared as a supporting track to 'Army Of Me', the first single from *Post*, and a version billed as 'Sweet Sweet Intuition', recorded at the Royal Festival Hall in London, also appears as a B-side to 'It's Oh So Quiet'.

A relatively sparse, restrained track musically, 'Sweet Intuition' finds Björk setting out in characteristically bald and nuance-free terms her declared life philosophy that instinct and impulse are all in art and, indeed, life. It's nevertheless a highly charming and likeable piece of outspoken electro-polemic, even if the shrilly emphasized chorus of "Fuck logic, fuck logic" tended to militate somewhat against excessive radio play.

24 Verandi

An Icelandic language track from the *Vespertine* sessions that failed to make its way on to the album, and possibly was never intended to, 'Verandi' surfaced as a backing track on 'Hidden Place', the first single from the album.

'Verandi' approximately translates from Icelandic as 'Human Condition' or 'State Of Being' and the song appears to be about subduing, while sensually enjoying, sexual desire. In a breathless,

25 Visur Vatnsenda-Rosu

'Visur Vatnsenda-Rosu"' is a traditional Icelandic song that translates as "Songs Of Watersend Rose" and was originally recorded by Björk in 1994 for inclusion on *Chansons Des Mers Froides* or *Songs From The Cold Seas*, an album by French composer Hector Zazou that also featured Jane Siberry, Suzanne Vega and John Cale.

The spectral, echoing song, reminiscent of alien-folk Irish band Clannad, tells the tale of a love tragically curtailed and the eternal hurt that results. Björk and Guy Sigsworth originally attempted, unsuccessfully, to record the original choral arrangement of the song, but were forced to settle for a sparse harp/vocal version. Zazou himself later remixed the track, which saw the light of day as a backing track to the 'Possibly Maybe' single from *Post*.

Singles,
B-sides and
side projects

CHRONOLOGY

1965

On November 21, Björk Gudmundsdóttir is born to electrical engineer and union leader Gudmundur Gunnarsson and his wife Hildur Hauksdóttir in Reykjavik.

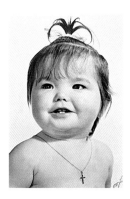

1968

Her parents divorce and Björk spends her childhood happily flitting between the two households. Her mother marries Sævar Árnason, the guitarist in a local blues band named Pops, who helps to nurture Björk's interest in music.

1977

After arousing the interest of local record label Fálkinn by singing 'I Love To Love' by UK disco singer Tina Charles on a Reykjavik radio station, Björk records her eponymous debut album at the age of eleven, helped by her step-father and his musician friends. Featuring a whimsical cover of the Beatles' 'Fool On The Hill' plus traditional songs and nursery rhymes, *Björk* sells five thousand copies and goes gold in Iceland.

1979

Björk joins a succession of local Reykjavik bands, including all-girl punk band Spit And Snot and experimental jazz outfit Exodus. She joins Tappi Tíkarrass ("Cork The Bitch's Ass") then finally the arty, post-punk Kukl, with whom she records two albums and tours Europe, with Crass.

1986

Kukl split and Björk marries local musician Thór Eldon and on June 8 gives birth to a son, Sindri. With friends, they form an art movement, Bad Taste Ltd, with a musical wing called The Sugarcubes.

1988

The Sugarcubes sign to London independent debut label One Little Indian. Their debut single 'Birthday' is greeted with critical acclaim and made single of the week in British weekly music paper *Melody Maker*. The Sugarcubes release their first album, *Life's Too Good*, tour the world and sell half-a-million copies.

1989

The Sugarcubes' release a second album, *Here Today, Tomorrow Next Week!*, but critics turn on the band's rowdy, trumpet-playing co-vocalist Einar Örn and the album performs disappointingly.

1990

Björk takes a break from The Sugarcubes to record a mostly Icelandic language album of traditional and folk standards, *Gling-Gló*, with Icelandic jazz musicians the Trio Gudmandar Ingólfssonar.

1991

Developing a growing interest in acid house music, Björk contacts Manchester acid house band 808 State and appears on two songs on their album *Ex:El*.

1992

Although riven by internal tensions, The Sugarcubes record a third album, *Stick Around For Joy*. They tour America with U2, and then split.

1993

Björk moves to London and works with Soul II Soul producer Nellee Hooper to record her first adult solo album, *Debut*, which is heavily influenced by contemporary club rhythms and the techno scene. It is released in July and reaches number 3 in the UK chart and number 61 in America.

1994

Björk is voted Best International Female Artist and Best International Newcomer at the BRIT Awards, where she sings the Rolling Stones' '(I Can't Get No) Satisfaction" with PJ Harvey. She writes "Bedtime Story' for Madonna but declines to sing the song as a duet, then flies to the Bahamas to record the follow-up to *Debut*.

1995

Post, Björk's second solo album, is released in June and reaches number 2 in the UK and number 32 in America. The album spawns her biggest hit, a cover of a 1940's show tune called 'It's Oh So Quiet'. The song nearly becomes a Christmas number one, partly due to an all-singing, all-dancing video by filmmaker Spike Jonze. Björk begins a romance with British drum'n'bass musician Goldie.

1996

A stressed-out Björk physically attacks a journalist, Julie Kaufman, at Bangkok Airport, then later apologises. In November, tragedy strikes when an obsessed Florida-based fan, Ricardo Lopez, is offended by Björk's relationship with Goldie on racist grounds. He posts a letter bomb to Björk's home in London, then videos himself committing suicide while listening to her music. The bomb is intercepted by police.

1997

Björk travels to Spain with Mark Bell of Leeds techno band LFO to record her third album, *Homogenic*. Musically the album is an attempt to render the fractured, volatile geography of Iceland, while the lyrics deal with her failed relationship with Goldie. *Homogenic*, Björk's most intense and confessional album to date, is released in November and charts at number 4 in the UK and number 28 in America. Björk quits London and returns to Reykjavik.

1999

Danish filmmaker Lars Von Trier contacts Björk and asks her to star in his movie *Dancer In The Dark*, about a doomed Czech immigrant woman in America with an abiding love for stage and film musicals. Björk refuses, and then relents. Filming begins in Sweden then transfers to Denmark, with Björk also composing the film's soundtrack. There are intense disagreements between the director and the singer.

2000

With filming on *Dancer In The Dark* completed, Björk begins work on her next studio album, which is provisionally called *Domestica*, and becomes obsessed with laptop electronica, recording in Iceland, Spain and New York.

At the Cannes Film Festival in May, *Dancer In The Dark* is awarded the Palme D'Or, the ultimate prize at the festival, and Björk is given the same award for Best Actress. At the subsequent press conference, she announces that she intends never to act again.

Dancer In The Dark goes on public release in September to extremely mixed reviews and Björk releases the soundtrack album *Selmasongs*, including a duet with Radiohead singer Thom Yorke.

2001

At the Academy Awards ceremony in March, Björk performs 'I've Seen It All' from *Dancer In The Dark* wearing her soon-to-be-famous swan dress but misses out on the Oscar for Best Song.

August sees Björk release her fourth adult solo album, by now called *Vespertine*. It is acclaimed as her most intimate and accomplished work to date and gives Björk her first US album chart Top 20 placing.

2002

In April, Björk announces that she is expecting her second child, by New York performance artist Matthew Barney.

DISCOGRAPHY

Björk is highly prolific and also the queen of the remix, and this discography does not claim to be remotely definitive. For this, we strongly recommend the brilliantly exhaustive discography section of her official website, **www.björk.com**, which lists all official releases and also major bootlegs. The fansite **www.alwaysontherun.net/björk** is excellent on obscurities plus the more arcane features of Björk's live repertoire, and also provides translations for most of her Icelandic lyrics.

The following basic discography thus lists all of Björk's solo single and album releases to date. The singles section covers UK releases only, although most main tracks were also released simultaneously in the US. The albums listings cover both UK and US releases. Catalogue numbers are for the CD format, and highest chart positions are given throughout.

SINGLES

'HUMAN BEHAVIOUR'
'Human Behaviour', 'Human Behaviour (Close To Human mix)', 'Human Behaviour (Underworld mix)', 'Human Behaviour (Dom T mix), 'Human Behaviour (Bassheads mix)'.
UK: One Little Indian 112TP7CD, June 1993. Chart: No 36.

'VENUS AS A BOY'
CD1: 'Venus As A Boy (edit)', 'Venus As A Boy (Mykaell Riley mix)', 'There's More To Life Than This (non-toilet mix)', 'Violently Happy (domestic mix)'.
UK: One Little Indian 122TP7CD, August 1993.

CD2: 'Venus As A Boy (7" dream mix)', Stigdu Mig', 'The Anchor Song (Black Dog mix)', 'I Remember You'.
UK: One Little Indian 122TP7CDL, August 1993. Chart: No 29.

'PLAY DEAD' (Björk and David Arnold)
'Play Dead', 'Play Dead (Tim Simenon orchestral remix)' 'Play Dead (Tim Simenon 12" remix)', 'Play Dead (Tim Simenon instrumental remix)', 'End Titles/Play Dead'.
UK: Island Records 862621-2, October 1993. Chart: No 12.

'BIG TIME SENSUALITY'
CD1: 'Big Time Sensuality', 'Sidasta Eg', 'Glóra', 'Come To Me (Black Dog mix)'.
UK: One Little Indian 132TP7CD, November 1993.

CD2: 'Big Time Sensuality (Fluke minimix)', 'Big Time Sensuality (Dom T big time club mix)', 'Big Time Sensuality (Justin Robertson Lionrock wigout vox mix)', 'Big Time Sensuality (Morales def radio mix)', Big Time Sensuality (Fluke magimix)', 'Big Time Sensuality (Justin Robertson pranksters joyride mix)', 'Big Time Sensuality (Fluke moulimix)'.
UK: One Little Indian 132TP7CDL, November 1993. Chart: No 17.

'VIOLENTLY HAPPY'
CD1: 'Violently Happy', 'The Anchor Song (acoustic)', 'Come To Me (acoustic)', 'Human Behaviour (acoustic)'.
UK: One Little Indian 142TP7CD, March 1994.

CD2: 'Violently Happy (Fluke even-tempered mix)', 'Violently Happy (Massey long mix)', 'Violently Happy (Masters At Work 12" mix)', 'Violently Happy (12" Nellee Hooper mix)', 'Violently Happy (Fluke well-tempered mix)', 'Violently Happy (Massey other mix)', 'Violently Happy (vox dub)'.
UK: One Little Indian 142TP7CDL, March 1994. Chart: No 13.

'ARMY OF ME'
CD1: 'Army Of Me', 'Cover Me', 'You've Been Flirting Again (Icelandic version)', 'Sweet Intuition'.
UK: One Little Indian 162TP7CD, April 1995.

CD2: 'Army Of Me (Aba All-Stars mix)', 'Army Of Me (Massey mix)', 'Army Of Me (featuring Skunk Anansie)', Army Of Me (Instrumental Aba All-Stars mix)'.
UK: One Little Indian 162TP7CDL, April 1995. Chart: No 10.

'ISOBEL'
CD1: 'Isobel', 'Charlene', 'I Go Humble', Venus As A Boy (harp mix)'.
UK: One Little Indian 172TP7CD, August 1995.

CD2: 'Isobel', 'Isobel (Deodato mix)', 'Isobel (Siggtriplet blunt mix)', 'Isobel's Lonely Heart (Goldie remix)'.
UK: One Little Indian 172TP7CDL, August 1995. Chart: No 23.

'IT'S OH SO QUIET'
CD1: 'It's Oh So Quiet', 'You've Been Flirting Again (Flirt Is A Promise mix)' 'Hyperballad (Over The Edge mix)', 'Sweet Sweet Intuition (Exclusive remix)'.
UK: One Little Indian 182TP7CD, November 1995.

CD2: 'It's Oh So Quiet', 'Hyperballad (Brodsky Quartet version)', 'Hyperballad (Girl's blouse mix)', 'My Spine'.
UK: One Little Indian 182TP7CDL, November 1995. Chart: No 4.

'HYPERBALLAD'
CD1: 'Hyperballad', 'Hyperballad (Robin Hood mix)', 'Hyperballad (Stomp mix)', 'Hyperballad (Fluke mix)', 'Hyperballad (Subtle abuse mix)', 'Hyperballad (Tee's freeze mix)'.
UK: One Little Indian 192TP7CD, February 1996.

CD2: 'Hyperballad', 'Isobel (Carcass mix), 'Cover Me (Plaid mix)', 'Hyperballad (Towa Tei remix)'.
UK: One Little Indian 192TP7CDL, February 1996. Chart: No 8.

'POSSIBLY MAYBE'
CD1: 'Possibly Maybe', 'Possibly Maybe (Lucy mix)', 'Possibly Maybe (Calcutta Cyber Cafe mix)', 'Possibly Maybe (Dallas Austin mix)'.
UK: One Little Indian 193TP7CD, November 1996.

CD2: 'Cover Me (Dillinja mix)', 'One Day (Trevor Morais mix)', 'Possibly Maybe (Calcutta Cyber Café dub mix)', 'I Miss You (Photek mix)'.
UK: One Little Indian 193TP7CL, November 1996.

CD3: 'Big Time Sensuality (Plaid mix)', 'Vísur Vatnsenda-Rósu', 'Possibly Maybe (live)', 'Hyperballad (Over The Edge mix live)'.
UK: One Little Indian 193TP7CDT, November 1996. Chart: No 13.

'I MISS YOU'
CD1: 'I Miss You', 'I Miss You (Dobie's Rub part 2 mix)', 'I Miss You (Darren Emerson underwater mix)', 'Karvel'.
UK: One Little Indian 194TP7CD, February 1997.

CD2: 'I Miss You (Dobie's Rub part 1 mix)', Hyperballad (LFO mix)', 'Violently Happy (live)', Headphones (Mika Vainio remix)'.
UK: One Little Indian, 194TP7CDL, February 1997. Chart: No 36.

'JÓGA'
CD1: 'Jóga', 'Jóga (string and vocal mix)', 'Jóga (buzz water mix)', 'All Is Full Of Love (Choice mix)'.
UK: One Little Indian 202TP7CD, September 1997.

CD2: 'Jóga', 'Sod Off', 'Immature', 'So Broken'.
UK: One Little Indian 202TP7CDL, September 1997.

CD3: 'Jóga', 'Jóga (Alec Empire mix)', 'Jóga (Alec Empire digital hardcore mix 1)', 'Jóga (Alec Empire digital hardcore mix 2)'.
UK: One Little Indian 202TP7CDX, September 1997.
Did not chart.

'BACHELORETTE'

CD1: 'Bachelorette', 'My Snare', 'Scary', 'Bachelorette (Howie spread mix)'.
UK: One Little Indian 212TP7CD, December 1997.

CD2: 'Bachelorette (Mark Bell optimism remix)' 'Bachelorette (Mark Bell zip remix)', 'Bachelorette (Mark Bell blue remix)', 'Bachelorette'.
UK: One Little Indian 212TP7CDLX, December 1997.

CD3: 'Bachelorette (RZA remix)', 'Bachelorette (Alec hypermodern jazz remix)', 'Bachelorette (Alec Empire the ice princess and the killer whale remix)', 'Bachelorette (Grooverider jeep remix)'.
UK: One Little Indian 212TP7CDX, December 1997. Chart: No 21.

'HUNTER'

CD1: 'Hunter', 'All Is Full Of Love (In Love with Funkstorung mix)', 'Hunter (u-ziq remix)'.
UK: One Little Indian 222TP7CD, October 1998.

CD2: 'Hunter', 'Hunter (State of Bengal remix)', 'Hunter (Skothus remix)'.
UK: One Little Indian 222TP7CDL, October 1998.

CD3: 'Hunter' (mood swing remix)', 'So Broken (DJ Krust remix)', 'Hunter (live)'.
UK: One Little Indian 222TP7CDX, October 1998. Chart: No 44.

'ALARM CALL'

CD1: 'Alarm Call', 'Alarm Call (rhythmic phonetics mix)', 'Alarm Call (Bjeck mix)'.
UK: One Little Indian 232TP7CD, November 1998.

CD2: 'Alarm Call (potage du jour mix)', 'Alarm Call (French edit)', 'Alarm Call (French dub)'.
UK: One Little Indian 232TP7CDL, November 1998.

CD3: 'Alarm Call (phunk you mix)', 'Alarm Call (gangsta mix)', 'Alarm Call (locked mix)'.
UK: One Little Indian 232TP7CDX, November 1998. Chart: No 33.

'ALL IS FULL OF LOVE'

CD1: 'All Is Full Of Love (video version)', 'All Is Full Of Love (Funkstorung mix)', 'All Is Full Of Love (strings mix)'.
UK: One Little Indian 242TP7CD, June 1999.

CD2: 'All Is Full Of Love', 'All Is Full Of Love (Plaid mix)', 'All Is Full Of Love (Guy Sigsworth mix)'.
UK: One Little Indian 242TP7CDI, June 1999. Chart: No 24.

'HIDDEN PLACE'

CD1: 'Hidden Place', 'Generous Palmstroke', 'Verandi'.
UK: One Little Indian 332TP7CD, August 2001.

CD2: 'Hidden Place (acapella version)', 'Mother Heroic', 'Foot Soldier'.
UK: One Little Indian 332TP7CDL. Chart: No 21.

'PAGAN POETRY'

CD1: 'Pagan Poetry (video edit)', 'Pagan Poetry (Matthew Herbert handshake mix)', 'Aurora (Opiate version)'.
UK: One Little Indian 352TP7CD, November 2001.

CD2: 'Pagan Poetry', 'Domestica', 'Batabid'.
UK: One Little Indian 352TP7CDL, November 2001. Chart: No 38.

'COCOON'

CD1: 'Cocoon', 'Pagan Poetry (music box version), 'Sun In My Mouth'.
UK: One Little Indian 322TP7CD, March 2002.

CD2: 'Cocoon', 'Aurora (music box version)', 'Amphibian'.
UK: One Little Indian 322TP7CDL, March 2002. Chart: No 35.

ALBUMS

BJÖRK

'Arabadrengurinn', 'Búkolla', 'Alta Mira', 'Jóhannes Kjarvalv', 'Fúsi Hreindyr', 'Himnaför', 'Óliver', 'Álfur Út Úr Hól', 'Músastiginn', 'Bænin'.
Iceland: Fálkinn Records FA006, December 1977.

GLING-GLÓ

'Gling-Gló', 'Luktar-Gvendur', 'Kata Rokkar', 'Pabbi Minn', 'Brestir Og Brak', 'Ástartöfrar', 'Bella Símamær', 'Litli Tónlistarmadurinn', 'Pad Sést Ekki Sætari Mey', 'Bílavísur', 'Tondeleyo', 'Ég Veit el Hvad Skal Segja', 'Í Dansi Med Pér', 'Börnin Vid Tjörnina', 'Ruby Baby', 'I Can't Help Loving That Man'.
Iceland: Smekkleysa Records SM27, 1990.

DEBUT

'Human Behaviour', 'Crying', 'Venus As A Boy', 'There's More To Life Than This', 'Like Someone In Love', 'Big Time Sensuality', 'One Day', 'Aeroplane', 'Come To Me', 'Violently Happy', 'The Anchor Song'.
* 'Play Dead' was added to later reissues of the album.
UK: One Little Indian TPLP31CD, July 1993. Chart: No 3.
US: Elektra 61468-2, July 1993. Chart: No 61.

POST

'Army Of Me', 'Hyper-ballad', 'The Modern Things', 'It's Oh So Quiet', 'Enjoy', 'You've Been Flirting Again', Isobel', 'Possibly Maybe', 'I Miss You', 'Cover Me', 'Headphones'.
UK: One Little Indian TPLP51CD, June 1995. Chart: No 2.
US: Elektra 617402, June 1995. Chart: No32.

TELEGRAM

'Possibly Maybe', 'Hyperballad', 'Enjoy', 'My Spine', 'I Miss You', 'Isobel', 'You've Been Flirting Again', 'Cover Me', 'Army Of Me', 'Headphones'.
UK: One Little Indian TPLPCD51T, November 1996.
US: Elektra 61897, January 1997. Chart: No 66.

HOMOGENIC

'Hunter', 'Jóga', 'Unravel', 'Bachelorette', 'All Neon Like', '5 Years', 'Immature', 'Alarm Call', 'Pluto', 'All Is Full Of Love'.
UK: One Little Indian TPLP71CD, September 1997. Chart: No 4.
US: Elektra 62061, September 1997. Chart: No 28.

SELMASONGS

'Overture', 'Cvalda', 'I've Seen It All', 'Scatterheart', 'In The Musicals', '107 Steps', 'New World'.
UK: One Little Indian TPLP151CD, September 2000.
US: Elekta, 62533-2, September 2000. Chart: No 41.

VESPERTINE

'Hidden Place', 'Cocoon', 'It's Not Up To You', 'Undo', 'Pagan Poetry', 'Frosti', 'Aurora', 'An Echo, A Stain', 'Sun In My Mouth', 'Heirloom', 'Harm Of Will', 'Unison'.
UK; One Little Indian TPLP101CD, August 2001. Chart: No 8.
US: Elektra 62653, August 2001. Chart: No 19.

INDEX